# Roadside Guide
to the
# Colorado Mountains:
# Interstate 25 Skylines

TEXT AND PHOTOGRAPHY BY H. JOSEPH MILLIGAN

WITH A FOREWORD BY JOHN FIELDER

WESTCLIFFE PUBLISHERS, INC., ENGLEWOOD, COLORADO

Published by:  Westcliffe Publishers, Inc.
               2650 South Zuni Street
               Englewood, Colorado 80110

Publisher:                John Fielder
Editors:                  Pattie Coughlin, Dougald MacDonald
Design and typography:    Joe Milligan
Cover design:             Joe Milligan,  Amy Duenkel

Pulisher's Cataloging in Publication
     (Prepared by Quality Books Inc.)

Milligan, H.Joseph.  Roadside Guide to the Colorado Mountains:
Interstate 25 Skylines / text and photography by H. Joseph Milligan
     p. cm.
     Includes index.
     LCCN: 95-71149
     ISBN 0-9647422-0-4

     1. Mountains—Colorado–Pictorial works. 2. Interstate 25—Pictorical works. 3. Colorado—Description and travel.  I. Title.  II. Interstate 25 skylines.

F774.3.M55 1996          917.8804'33
                         QBI96-20266

*To Grace Elaine Milligan, my grandmother,*
————————    *who taught me to read*    ————————
*and to love books*

# *Table of Contents*

## CHAPTER 3 • SOUTHERN I-25: NEW MEXICO TO COLORADO SPRINGS

# *Foreword*

Believe it or not, I need this book as much as you do. Though I have been photographing Colorado's mountains for almost twenty five years—and make my living doing so—I still cannot identify most of the mountains I see from Colorado's highways.

Perhaps it's because I prefer photographing mountains up close, or because I am in too much of a hurry driving to the trailhead to notice which one is which. I know that I am always left with an empty feeling when I look out the car window, see the glory of a range of peaks in the warm light of sunset, and realize that I don't know the names of the mountains. I know that I've probably been on top of or just below those mountains, probably even photographed them, but, from this angle or that, I just can't figure out which one is which from the highway.

What a relief to have Joe Milligan come along! Now I can avoid the embarrassment when I can't answer questions from friends and family: "John, if anyone would know, it would be you. What's the name of that peak?" And not only will I now be able to identify every mountain I see, but I also can talk about the history of each peak, thanks to the useful information Joe has collected.

If for nothing else, Colorado is known for its mountains. I have photographed around the West and decided to settle in Colorado because it contained the most beautiful ranges in the world. From the Sangre de Cristos in the south to the great Front Range and Rocky Mountain National Park farther north, the spectacle of the mountain world is unsurpassed here, and so much of it is available to see and enjoy from our network of highways. Though I hope you will ultimately have the chance to visit these places on foot, to be able to touch them and photograph them as I do, this book at least will give you the opportunity to learn what's out there to explore, and certainly will allow you to recognize them as I always should have.

John Fielder
Englewood, Colorado

# *Preface*

Why are we so fascinated with mountains? They seem to raise within us a stirring, a longing to return to them again and again. Our curiosity and attraction never seems to be quenched. Their solitude comforts us, their dizzying heights excite us, and their massive presence awes us. Below them we stand in humble admiration. Intriguing and inspiring, they sometimes deeply move us and nearly always exhilarate us.

There seems to be a little bit of the explorer born in each of us. We want to know what's around the next corner or what's up ahead. Our thirst for knowledge leads us to be curious about our surroundings, and part of knowing our surroundings is familiarity with the names of things around us. When we can name an object or feature, we feel more secure in our world.

I am always curious about the names of mountains. This is especially true as I drive, because I can cover territory quickly and I can ponder many peaks and their names. I realized how handy it would be to have a map or book that showed the mountains and peaks from a "roadside view," and not a "bird's eye view." This idea gradually evolved into the PeakFinders™ Guide.

Like most *new* ideas, it wasn't new at all. In the 1960s and again in the 1970s, this idea has been tried in different ways. In 1962 Louisa Ward Arps and the Colorado Mountain Club produced a folder of panoramic drawings depicting part of the Colorado front range from downtown Denver titled *Front Range Panorama* . This collection of drawings clearly identified the mountains as seen from Denver. It has been out of print for many years. In the early 1970s an extraordinary Colorado mountain climber and writer by the name of Bob Ormes produced a series of books on a similar principle. Mr. Ormes traveled around Colorado photographing the mountains from prominent locations. He then traced the outline of the photographs, added text with his typewriter to the mountain outlines, and self-published the books. Without the use of computers, databases, and desktop publishing, this was a huge undertaking, requiring several years to complete. The books have also been out of print for many years.

Today, with portable computers, digital maps, and state-of-the-art software, it was possible to re-create Mr. Ormes' concept, so we can discover anew our wonderful Colorado mountains.

So, in your Colorado travels, during a cool early morning, as the alpenglow turns the mountains brilliant pink, if you happen to see a fellow alongside the road gazing at the view—stop and say hello. It just might be me, and we can chat about the mountains and enjoy the spectacular views.

Joe Milligan

Colorado Springs, Colorado

# *Acknowledgments*

What a tremendous effort it was to put this book together. Countless people have, in one way or another, helped me bring it to completion. Many organizations also assisted with the preparation of this project, including the United States Geological Survey, the United States Board on Geographic Names, and the Colorado Mountain Club.

Numerous authors have written about Colorado place names, and their research and writings have been a tremendous help. Please see the bibliography at the back of the book for a complete list.

I am indebted to the following people for their help, assistance, suggestions, and moral support.

First, this book would never have been written without the love, encouragement, and *help* of my wife and soul-mate, Marcy. Her heart is truly as large as any Colorado mountain.

My humble gratitude and appreciation go to Mike Foster and Joe Kramarsic. These fellow authors and Colorado Mountain Club members spent countless hours reviewing the technical content. This book could not have been completed without their tremendous help.

Thanks to Ray Sterner at the Johns Hopkins University Applied Physics Laboratory for generating the shaded-relief map.

To my fellow members of the Community Enterprise Lending Initiative (CELI) program: Rich Brockman, Al Brown, James Bruno, Joanie McNiece, Sandy Powell, Ginny Ruths, Paige Van DenAardweg, and Terry Zebarth—thank you. These energetic entrepreneurs helped me turn an avocation into a vocation. Their shrewd and astute business advice has been indispensable.

My thanks go to the Colorado Independent Publishers Association (CIPA) for providing me with assistance, knowledge, and new friends.

Thanks to Greg Walters and Jim Roth  at Sharp Art, Inc., for help with refining the cover design.

Thanks to Warren Jokinen, Macintosh power user and computer guru.

And thanks also to Barbara, Brad, Rick, and Ryan, who endured the sometimes painful process of living under the same roof with a writer.

# Introduction

Ellingwood Ridge  La Plata Peak

# Introduction

"Because they are there." PeakFinders™ guidebooks are dedicated to satisfying the curiosity and wonder we all have for the spectacular Colorado mountains. Intended for visitors and residents alike, these books will help you quickly identify mountain skylines and peaks throughout the state from major roads, scenic overlooks, and rural highways.

PeakFinders *Roadside Guide to the Colorado Mountains: Interstate 25 Skylines* identifies the mountains along the front ranges of Colorado as seen from Interstate 25.

With so many peaks in the Rocky Mountains, it can be difficult to identify each one. Topographic maps help, but most people do not know how to interpret these technical maps which depict a "bird's-eye" view instead of a "person's-eye" view. Besides, it's impractical to carry the dozens of topographic maps needed to chart Colorado's front ranges.

Your PeakFinders Guide is a convenient reference to the mountains of Colorado. You can identify the mountains you see along the road without consulting bulky, expensive, and hard-to-use topographical maps. The book also gives you history, lore, and facts on the mountains, all in one easy-to-use volume.

## About the Book and Photographs

This book shows the major mountains and landmarks seen from Interstate 25 in Colorado. All major peaks and landmarks are identified. To reduce clutter in the photographs, many smaller features may not be identified.

The photographs have been electronically manipulated to enhance their reproduction, and some are composites of several images. The author takes full responsibility for any errors or inaccuracies that exist in this work. If you believe that you have found an error or inaccuracy, please write to me in care of the publisher and enclose copies of any supporting documents and/or references.

Early road travelers in Colorado, 1926
(*photo courtesy of W. R. Studhalter*)

# How to Use your PeakFinders™ Guide

The book is arranged by mile marker to make it convenient and easy to locate your position. Simply turn to the page of the book that reflects the mile marker closest to your current location.

At the top of each page is a photograph of the skyline, annotated with the names of the major mountains and landmarks that you see from your current location. Simply match the mountain you see on the skyline to the mountain you see in the photograph. In some locations, a wide-angle panorama is followed by a page with a close-up photograph, where more detail on individual features can be identified.

Background information on selected mountains or landmarks is listed below the photographs. Information for individual mountains may be spread across many pages. Refer to the index for a list of each page that a mountain appears on.

On the right side of many pages is a map. It depicts your location (the little car on the map), what direction to look, and the area you are seeing. Figure 1 demonstrates how the map works. In this example, you are at mile marker 220, just north of Denver. You are looking to the west-northwest, toward the Arapaho Peaks.

Be advised that you may see the same basic view for many miles. In other words, *the view at mile marker 220, to the west-northwest, may be very similar to the view you see from mile marker 230 or 210.* In this case, only one view and one mile marker is presented.

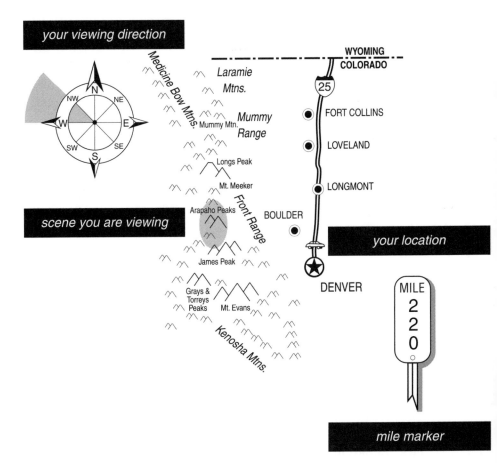

Figure 1. How the maps work

## How to Identify Mountain Skylines

It can be very difficult to identify mountains. Although the mountains and landmarks are anchored in one position, they appear to move as your location changes. The skyline is not a cardboard cutout. It is a dynamic, complex view. The same mountain will look different from the north, from the west, or from the southeast.

As you drive along, try pulling over and looking behind you. The mountain that you passed 15 miles ago will look quite different now. The mountain's silhouette changes as your angle to it changes, and the elevation of your viewing location also influences the skyline.

One aid to identifying mountains is to visualize them and their neighbors in three dimensions. By identifying prominent features, you can interpolate how those features relate to the mountains as they turn three-dimensionally in your mind's eye. If you select a mountain on the skyline and a familiar feature in the foreground, such as a foothill or a man-made landmark, you can then shift the image in your mind's eye to help in the identification of the mountain in question.

Another helpful practice is knowing and keeping track of your orientation. Knowing if you are north, west, or southeast of a peak will assist you in tracking each mountain. Practice will increase your accuracy and allow you to readily identify the mountains you see on the skyline.

Locations for the photographs in this guide have been carefully selected to show the peaks and landmarks from a "middle point" or in their most characteristic view.

## Visibility and Mountains

We all know that weather can affect visibility. During rain and snow, visibility can be reduced to less than a mile. The time of day is also a key element. Visibility is best early in the morning. As the day progresses, the contrast of the light becomes less and less as the sun climbs higher in the sky. Likewise, as the air temperature and humidity increase, the visibility decreases.

On a clear day in the early morning, you may be able to see more than one hundred miles. Under poor conditions, it may be difficult to discern an object only twenty-five miles away. When the conditions are very poor, you may be lucky to see an object five miles away.

 **Tidbits** – Throughout the book I have sprinkled small pieces of interesting information or related facts in what I call tidbits. When you see the compass symbol like the one to the left, you have found a tidbit. Be sure to read it for interesting additional information.

·2·

---

# Geography and Geology of the Colorado Mountains

# Geography of the Colorado Mountains

Traveling westward across Colorado's diverse terrain is a remarkable journey. Leaving the flat prairies of the high central plains, the visitor soon encounters the majestic peaks of the Rocky Mountains—the backbone of our continent and home to the Continental Divide. These shining mountains rise dramatically, marking an abrupt end to the Great Plains.

Colorado is home to 54 mountain peaks that rise over 14,000 feet (4,250 meters). There are only 68 peaks above 14,000 feet in the entire continental United States. More than 1,500 Colorado summits rise above 12,000 feet (3,658 meters).

## The Mountain Ecosystems

Within a day's drive, or a day's hike, you can visit the ecosystems of both the rolling plains and the frozen land of alpine tundra, more than two miles above sea level. Colorado truly is a diverse land of mountains and plains.

As you drive from plain to mountain top, you pass through the montane, subalpine, and alpine ecosystems. For each 1,000 feet (300 meters) of elevation that you gain, the temperature drops by about 3 degrees Fahrenheit or 1 degree Celsius. Geographically, this is equivalent to driving 600 miles (965 kilometers) northward toward the Arctic Circle. Therefore, a trip from sunny Colorado Springs to timberline on Pikes Peak, at an elevation of about 11,500 feet (3,500 meters), is the same as driving northward about 3,000 miles (4,800 kilometers).

Driving in the high Colorado mountains, the ecosystems that you pass through share many similarities with the ecosystems that you would see on a trip toward the Arctic. At the highest elevations, fragile tundra grows slowly, often taking 20 years to grow an inch. The summer is only about six to eight weeks long. The rest of the year is marked by snow, freezing temperatures, and strong winds.

## The Colorado Front Range

Nestled along the western edge of the Great Plains is the Colorado Front Range of the Rocky Mountains. It is so-named because travelers from the eastern plains were greeted with a view of these spectacular peaks, rising in grandeur at the "front" of the Rockies.

Common usage places the Front Range from Colorado Springs northward to Fort Collins, close to the Wyoming border. Technically, the Colorado Front Range is a smaller segment of the mountains that can be seen in this area—nine different ranges collectively known as the Front Range. Millions of years ago, deep within the bowels of the earth, a north-south-trending fold of hard rock pushed upward, causing the birth of the Front Range. It is theorized that the Ancestral Rocky Mountains contained a front range near the one we see today.

## Colorado Mountain Names

Colorado boasts more than 3,200 named summits. Thousands of unnamed summits, ridges, and high points also exist within the Colorado borders.

The origin of geographical names is a rich area of study. Many names came from early explorers, cartographers, and settlers. Other names of geographical features honor prominent persons and local residents. Regrettably, most of the original Native American names for Colorado's geographic features are lost.

Many mountains have been known by more than one name. Over the years, this led to confusion and disorganization. In 1890, the United States Board on Geographic Names was established to standardize geographic nomenclature.

The U.S. Board on Geographic Names does not name anything itself. The board merely accepts or rejects proposals for new names or changes to existing names, based upon its principles and policies. Primarily, the board rules on physical features and certain types of cultural features. However, the board will rule on any feature's name if asked to do so, or to settle disputes among individuals, groups, or organizations. The board also works closely with state name authorities and local governments toward the mission of standardization.

## Geographic Definitions

What exactly is a mountain? For that matter, how is a hill different from a mountain? And who decides? There are no set standards for determining what is a mountain and what is a hill. (The same can be said of other geographic terms, such as creek and river.) A twist of an old proverb says, "one man's hill is another man's mountain."

For some time, the United States Board on Geographic Names defined the difference between a hill and a mountain as 1,000 feet of local relief, but that definition fell into disuse by the early 1970s. Various agencies of the federal government may have definitions for their own specific applications, but there are no standards.

The United States Geological Survey (USGS) maintains a database of all geographic names, called the National Geographic Names Database (NGNDB). In this database are definitions for various classes of geographic features. The following classes are used in the Geographic Names Database and in this book:

**basin**  A natural depression or relatively low area enclosed by higher land. Geographic features in this class include sink, pit, amphitheater, and cirque.

**bench**  An area of relatively level land on the flank of an elevation such as a hill, ridge, or mountain, where the slope of the land rises on one side and descends on the opposite side.

**cliff**  A very steep slope. Geographic features in this class include bluff, crag, precipice, head, headland, nose, palisade, promontory, rim, and rimrock.

**gap**  A low point or opening between hills or mountains or in a ridge or mountain range. Geographic features in this group include pass, notch, water gap, wind gap, saddle, and col.

**glacier**  A body or stream of ice moving outward and downslope from an area of accumulation or an area of relatively permanent snow and ice on the top or side of a mountain or mountainous area. Geographic features include patch, snow patch, and icefield.

**pillar**  A vertical, often spire-shaped natural rock formation. Geographic features include pinnacle, chimney, monument, rock, and tower.

**ridge**  An elevation with a narrow, elongated crest that can be part of a hill or mountain. Geographic features in this class include rim, crest, cuesta, escarpment, hogback, and spur.

**summit** A prominent elevation rising above the surrounding level of the earth's surface (not including ridges and ranges). Geographic features in this class include hill, mountain, knob, butte, berg, colina, cone, volcano, cumbre, dome, head, knoll, mesa, meseta, mound, mount, peak, rock, sugar loaf, table, bald cerro, and horn.

## The Mountain Ranges of Colorado

The USGS defines a mountain range as a linear chain of hills or mountains that can be segmented into geological or geographical units. Because a mountain range is viewed relative to its surroundings, you can consider the entire Rocky Mountains as a range, compared with the plains to the east and the deserts to the west. Within the Rocky Mountains are many groupings of mountains that are considered unique and linear ranges, such as the Front Range, the Sawatch Range, the Culebra Range, and the Sangre de Cristo Range. Sometimes the name does not even contain the word "range," such as the Elk Mountains and the Wet Mountains, but a range is implied.

Many of the larger ranges can be further broken down into subranges or groupings of mountains and peaks, such as the Rampart Range, a subrange within the Front Range. Since there are no concrete parameters for segmenting ranges, this leads to some ranges having a local or common name, as well as the official name.

According to the USGS, there are more than 70 named mountain ranges in the great state of Colorado. Many groupings of hills and mountains can be divided into subranges. In this book, these subranges will be referred to as groups.

The following list attempts to assign a hierarchical order to the major Colorado ranges and subranges or groups. It includes USGS official names and local names that are, or at one time were, in common usage.

**Culebra Range**

**Elk Mountains**
  Anthracite Range
  Ruby Range
  West Elk Mountains
  Williams Mountains

**Elkhead Mountains**
  Sawtooth Range
  Williams Fork Mountains

**Front Range**
  Chicago Mountains
  Indian Peaks
  The Ironclads
  Kenosha Mountains
  Mummy Range
  Pikes Peak
  Platte River Mountains
  Rampart Range
  Tarryall Mountains

**Gore Range**

**Laramie Mountains**

**Medicine Bow Mountains**
  Rawahs

**Mosquito Range**

**Never Summer Mountains**

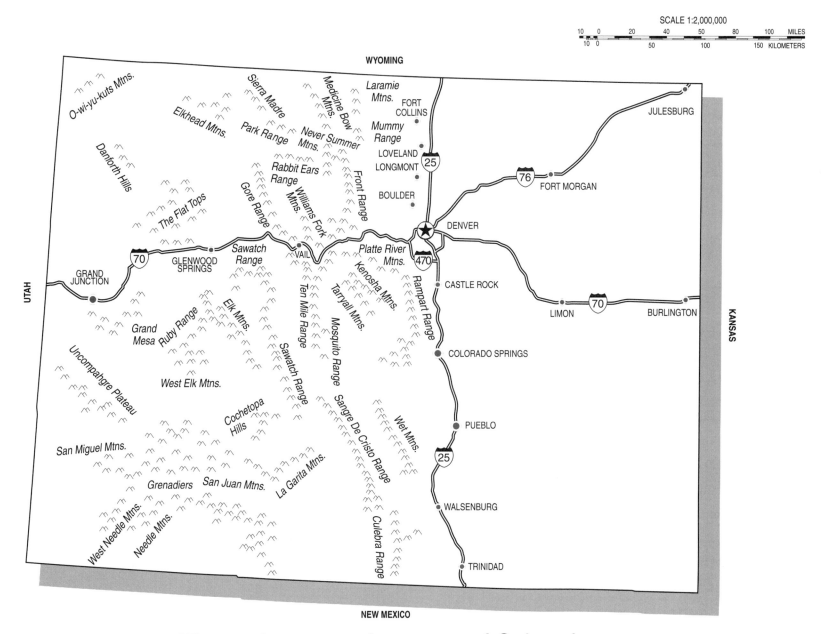

SCALE 1:2,000,000

WYOMING

O-wi-yu-kuts Mtns.

Sierra Madre

Medicine Bow Mtns.

Laramie Mtns.

FORT COLLINS

JULESBURG

Elkhead Mtns.

Park Range

Never Summer Mtns.

Mummy Range

LOVELAND

LONGMONT

25

76

FORT MORGAN

Danforth Hills

Rabbit Ears Range

Williams Fork Mtns.

Front Range

BOULDER

Gore Range

The Flat Tops

Sawatch Range

VAIL

Platte River Mtns.

★ DENVER

470

GLENWOOD SPRINGS

Kenosha Mtns.

Rampart Range

CASTLE ROCK

70

GRAND JUNCTION

Grand Mesa

Ruby Range

Elk Mtns.

Ten Mile Range

Tarryall Mtns.

70

LIMON

BURLINGTON

Mosquito Range

KANSAS

Uncompahgre Plateau

West Elk Mtns.

Sawatch Range

COLORADO SPRINGS

San Miguel Mtns.

Cochetopa Hills

Sangre De Cristo Range

Wet Mtns.

PUEBLO

25

Grenadiers

San Juan Mtns.

La Garita Mtns.

WALSENBURG

West Needle Mtns.

Needle Mtns.

Culebra Range

TRINIDAD

NEW MEXICO

UTAH

# The major mountain ranges of Colorado

**Park Range**

**Rabbit Ears Range**

**San Juan Mountains**

    Chalk Mountains

    Grassy Mountains

    Grenadier Range

    La Garita Mountains

    La Plata Mountains

    Mesa Mountains

    Needle Mountains

    Rico Mountains

    West Needle Mountains

**San Miguel Mountains**

**Sangre de Cristo Mountains**

**Sawatch Range**

    Collegiate Peaks
    The Seven Hermits

**Sierra Madre**

**Spanish Peaks**

**Tenmile Range**

**Uinta Mountains**

    O-wi-yu-kuts Mountains

**Wet Mountains**

The following is an alphabetical list of the official USGS mountain ranges in Colorado and the Colorado counties in which they are located.

| RANGE | COUNTIES |
| --- | --- |
| Ant Hills | Moffat |
| Anthracite Range | Gunnison |
| Badger Hills | Pueblo |
| Bare Hills | Fremont |
| Basaltic Hills | Conejos |
| Bear Springs Hills | Las Animas |
| Big Arroyo Hills | Las Animas |
| Black Hills | Las Animas |
| Bloom Hills | Otero, Las Animas |
| Chalk Mountains | Archuleta |
| Cochetopa Hills | Saguache |
| Culebra Range | Costilla, Huerfano, Las Animas |
| Danforth Hills | Moffat, Rio Blanco |
| East Sand Hills | Jackson |
| Elk Mountains | Pitkin, Gunnison, Eagle |
| Elkhead Mountains | Moffat, Routt |
| Escalante Breaks | Mesa |
| Front Range | Routt, Boulder, Clear Creek, El Paso, Fremont, Gilpin, Grand, Jefferson, Larimer, Teller |
| Gilsonite Hills | Rio Blanco |
| Gore Range | Eagle, Summit, Grand, Routt |
| Gorge Hills | Fremont |

| RANGE | COUNTIES | RANGE | COUNTIES |
|-------|----------|-------|----------|
| Grand Canyon Hills | Fremont | Rampart Range | Douglas, Teller, El Paso |
| Grassy Hills | San Miguel | Redlands, The | Mesa |
| Gray Hills | Rio Blanco, Moffat | Rico Mountains | Dolores |
| Grenadier Range | San Juan | Rosita Hills | Custer |
| Hooker Hills | Pueblo | Ruby Range | Gunnison |
| Indian Peaks | Boulder, Grand | San Juan Mountains | Archuleta, Mineral |
| Iron Springs Hills | Otero | San Luis Hills | Conejos, Costilla |
| Ironclads, The | Boulder | San Miguel Mountains | Dolores, San Miguel |
| La Garita Mountains | Mineral, Saguache | Sanford Hills | Pueblo |
| La Plata Mountains | Montezuma, La Plata | Sangre de Cristo Mountains | Costilla |
| Medicine Bow Mountains | Jackson, Larimer | Sawatch Range | Chaffee, Gunnison |
| Mesa Mountains | La Plata | Sawtooth Range | Routt |
| Mosquito Range | Lake | Seven Hermits, The | Eagle |
| Mummy Range | Larimer | Shale Hills | Otero |
| Needle Mountains | San Juan, La Plata | Sierra Madre | Jackson, Routt |
| Never Summer Mountains | Jackson, Grand, Larimer | Smith Hollow Hills | Las Animas |
| North Sand Hills | Jackson | Tarryall Mountains | Park |
| O-wi-yu-kuts Mountains | Moffat | Tenmile Range | Summit |
| Park Range | Jackson, Routt | Uinta Mountains | Moffat |
| Pawnee Hills | Weld | Ute Hills | Las Animas |
| Pete Hills | Las Animas | West Elk Mountains | Delta, Gunnison, Montrose |
| Pinon Hills | Conejos | West Needle Mountains | San Juan, La Plata |
| Platte River Mountains | Park | Wet Mountains | Custer |
| Poitrey Arroyo Hills | Las Animas | Williams Fork Mountains | Grand, Summit, Moffat, Routt |
| Puma Hills | Park | Williams Mountains | Pitkin |
| Rabbit Ears Range | Grand, Jackson | | |

# Geology of the Colorado Mountains

## The Rocky Mountains

The Rocky Mountains extend from above the Arctic Circle in Alaska south through Canada and the United States to New Mexico. The Rockies contain many mountain ranges—more than 100 distinct ranges in the United States alone. They comprise the longest chain of mountains in North America, at more than 3,000 miles (4,800 kilometers).

Running along the ridgetops of the Rockies is the Continental Divide, where the Pacific and Atlantic watersheds separate. Water falling as rain or snow on the west side of the divide eventually makes its way to the Pacific Ocean. Water falling on the east side of the divide eventually will make its way to the Atlantic Ocean. The Continental Divide runs completely across North America.

## Formation of the Rockies

The mountains we see in Colorado today are not the original Rocky Mountains. They are descendants of the original Rockies known as the Ancestral Rocky Mountains. About 300 million years ago, when the continental plates were in collision, the Ancestral Rockies raised skyward thousands of feet. This was called the Colorado Orogeny. Remnants of these early mountains can be found today along the Colorado Front Range. The tilted reddish sandstone rocks at the Garden of the Gods Park in Colorado Springs, Red Rocks Park outside of Denver, and the Boulder Flatirons are some examples.

The Ancestral Rockies were eroded by wind, rain, and ice to nothing more than rolling hills. Much of the debris was deposited onto the high plains of the west. Then, about 65 million years ago, another uplift began the formation of the current Rocky Mountains. Called the Laramide Orogeny, this uplift continued off and on until approximately 6 million years ago. This time was marked by periods of great erosion, volcanic eruptions, and regional uplifts.

## The Ice Age and Glaciers

During the great Ice Ages that occurred from 6 million to 10,000 years ago, glaciers formed in the high mountain valleys. Glaciers are created as the annual snowfall exceeds the amount of snowmelt each year. Gradually, this unmelted snow compresses and turns to ice. As the years go by, the ice grows into huge glaciers, often many thousands of feet thick.

As gravity tugged at the Rocky Mountain glaciers, they moved slowly down the mountains, carving and gouging them, steepening their sides, and sculpting bowl-shaped depressions called cirques.

As the alpine glaciers moved downward, they carried rock and debris as they went. About 14,000 years ago, when the glaciers began to melt and retreat back up the mountain sides, they deposited the boulders and debris that they had carried. The resulting low hills and ridges are called glacial moraines and can be found in many locations in Colorado.

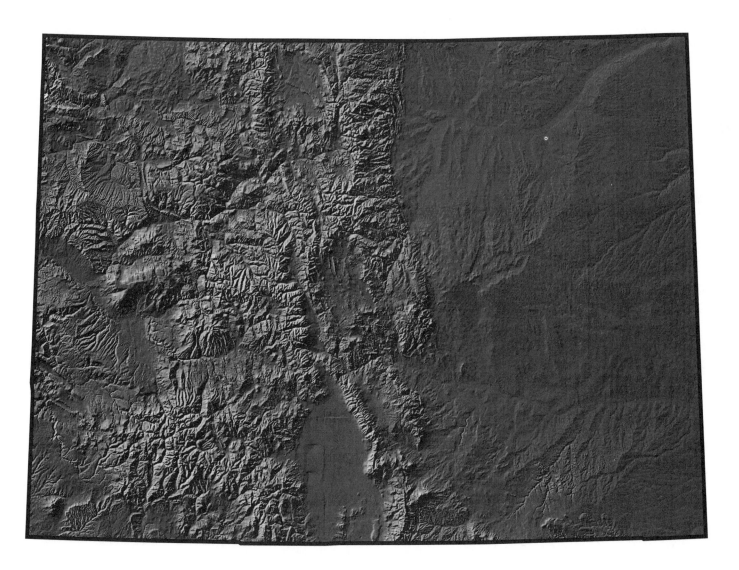

Map by Ray Sterner, Johns Hopkins University Applied Physics Laboratory

# Shaded-relief map of Colorado

Chapter 2 • Geography and Geology of the Colorado Mountains

The glaciers that occupied the Rocky Mountains enriched the landscape with breathtaking basins, high alpine valleys, and steep mountain peaks. Today in Colorado there are no glaciers. However, there are several permanent snowfields or "miniature" glaciers. Some of these have characteristics of larger glaciers, such as blue ice, crevasses, and deposit moraines along their margins and snout.

## Geographical Source Information

Since there are sometimes conflicting names, elevations, or origins of place names cited in various sources, I have chosen to cite United States Geological Survey (USGS) data and United States Board on Geographic Names (USBGN) whenever possible. However, sometimes the USGS or USBGN data does not exist or may be in error. In this case, I have used the source material deemed the most accurate. When a conflict exists that cannot be verified or validated, multiple sources are used and correct conclusions are left to the reader to resolve.

# Southern I-25: New Mexico to Colorado Springs

## TRIP HIGHLIGHTS

- Views of the Sangre de Cristo Range, the longest in the Rocky Mountains.

- Sweeping panoramas of the Culebra Range—one of the least traveled areas in Colorado.

- Fantastic views of the romantic Spanish Peaks, born of volcanic origins.

- Views of historic southern Colorado geological landmarks.

Raton Pass

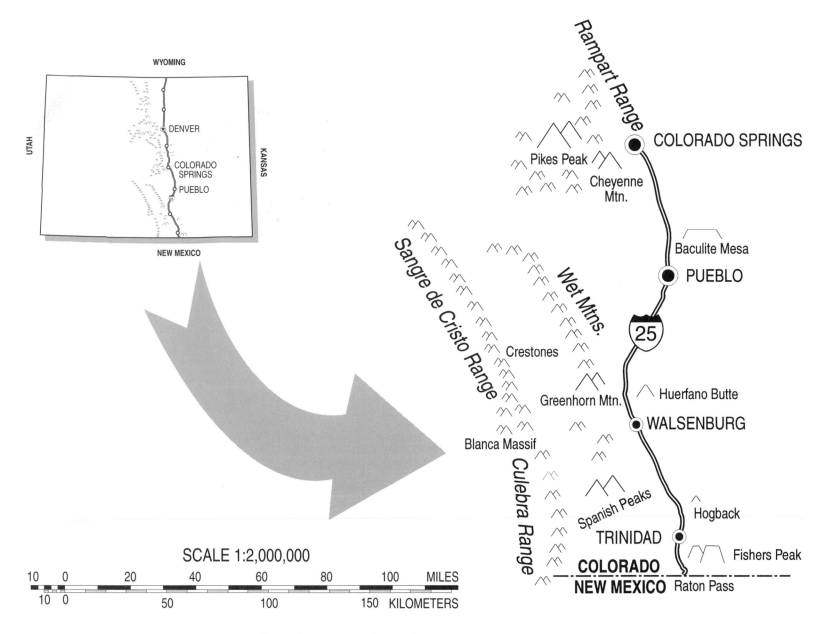

SCALE 1:2,000,000

Map of southern I-25 from the New Mexico border to Colorado Springs

This panorama looks toward the south side of Fishers Peak and the eastern end of Raton Mesa. It is taken from the scenic overlook just north of the New Mexico border, at mile marker 001. The view is to the northeast. Fishers Peak is 7 miles (11 km) in the distance. Note that the exit to this scenic overlook is accessible only from northbound I-25.

**Baldy** – 8,068 ft (2,459 m).

**Fishers Peak** – 9,627 ft (2,934 m). Historical lore suggests the original owners of the large Maxwell land grant moved one of their corner boundary markers from the original Fishers Peak—near Raton Pass or the mesa itself—north to Raton Peak, claiming it as Fishers Peak, which increased the size of their holdings by thousands of acres. Today, Fishers Peak is the common name associated with this majestic plateau and is marked accordingly on USGS maps.

**Berg** – 9,503 ft (2,909 m).

**Fishers Peak Mesa** – 9,625 ft (2,934 m). This summit, or a prominent point nearby, is probably the original Fishers Peak, named after Captain Waldemar Fischer, a Prussian-trained officer in command of an artillery battery during the Mexican War of 1846. (See also Fishers Peak.) Historical documents describe Captain Fischer becoming lost in the area and climbing this peak to establish his bearings. A shoulder of this great mesa is probably his high point. The German spelling of the name Fischer was dropped over the years in favor of the English spelling—Fisher.

**Raton Mesa** – 9,064 ft (2,276 m).

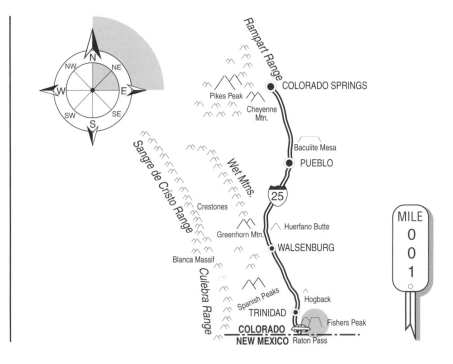

This sweeping panorama, covering this page and the next, is a view of the Culebra Range from the east. The mountains are about 32 miles (52 km) in the distance. The Culebra Range is probably the least-explored and least-traveled mountain range in Colorado. These pictures are taken from Starkville, exit 11, just south of Trinidad.

**State Line Peak** – 12,867 ft (3,922 m). Also known as Costilla Peak and Red Peak, this mountain sits on the Colorado-New Mexico border.

**Purgatoire Peak** – 13,676 ft (4,168 m). Named for the Purgatoire River which flows from here through Trinidad. The river originally was called *El Rio de Las Animas Perdidas en Purgatorio*, which means "the river of the lost souls in Purgatory," because several early Spanish explorers died near the river without receiving last rights.

**Vermejo Peak** – 13,723 ft (4,183 m). Named after Vermejo Creek, which was named for the reddish color of its water. Vermejo is from the Spanish *bermejo*, which means "a shade of red."

**Red Mountain** – 13,908 ft (4,239 m). Also called *Espinazo Rojo,* which means "red spine" in Spanish. Most likely named for its very long and distinctive east ridge.

**Culebra Peak** – 14,047 ft (4,282 m). *Culebra* is Spanish for "snake," and the peak takes its name from the winding Culebra Creek, which begins on the western slopes of the Culebras. The highest point in the Culebras, this is the southernmost peak over 14,000 feet in Colorado.

**Miranda Peak** – 13,468 ft (4,105 m). This peak is named for Guadalupe Miranda, who, with Charles Beaubien, received more than one million acres in a land grant from

Manuel Armijo, the New Mexico territorial governor, in 1841. A variant name—Peak N, comes from the peculiar N-shaped snowbank that can be seen on the mountainside in the spring.

**Lomo Liso Mountain** – 13,128 ft (4,001 m). *Lomo liso* is Spanish for "smooth back."

**Francisco Peak** – 13,135 ft (4,004 m). This name was granted by the Board on Geographic Names in 1972. The peak is named after Colonel John M. Francisco, who settled in the Colorado territory in 1839 and was a founding father of the town of La Veta.

**Beaubien Peak** – 13,184 ft (4,018 m). Named for Charles Beaubien (?-1864), who became one of the West's largest land owners, amassing close to 2.5 million acres. In a suspicious court transaction, he once bought a 50 percent stake in 1 million acres for a mere 100 dollars! (See also Miranda Peak.)

**De Anza Peak** – 13,333 ft (4,064 m). Also known as *Cono De Anza*. Named after Juan Bautista de Anza (1735-1788), a Spanish explorer and Mexican governor.

**Mariquita Peak** – 13,405 ft (4,086 m). *Mariquita* is the Spanish word for "ladybug." These small orange insects periodically gather near the summit in such numbers that rocks and short foliage become completely obscured.

Culebra Peak is the only Colorado peak over 14,000 feet that is completely surrounded by private property. Snow remains high on the peak all year, with the exception of about 10 weeks in late summer and early fall. The massive Spanish Peaks are about 30 miles (48 km) in the distance.

**Mount Maxwell** – 13,335 ft (4,065 m). Named after Lucine Bonaparte Maxwell (1818-1875), the husband of Luz Beaubien, who purchased from her father, Charles Beaubien, his share of the Beaubien and Miranda land grant. This land covered an area from the Culebra Range to east of Trinidad, and south almost to Taos, New Mexico.

**Cuatro Peak** – 13,487 ft (4,111 m). *Cuatro* is Spanish for the number "four." The mountain is so-named because, during the spring snow melt, a very clear Roman numeral IV can be seen on the mountain side. Also known as Quatro Peak.

**Trinchera Peak** – 13,517 ft (4,120 m). Named after Trinchera Creek. *Trinchera* is Spanish for "trench" or "entrenchment." Early settlers protected themselves from Indian attacks in such trenches. Many peaks in the Culebra Range are named after the rivers and creeks surrounding them. Trinchera, Culebra, Vermejo, and Purgatoire are just a few.

**Park Mountain** – 11,670 ft (3,557 m).

**West Spanish Peak** – 13,626 ft (4,153 m). The peaks have also been known as *Los Dos Hermanos,* meaning "the two brothers."

**East Spanish Peak** – 12,683 ft (3,866 m). The Spanish Peaks are southern Colorado's most conspicuous landmarks.

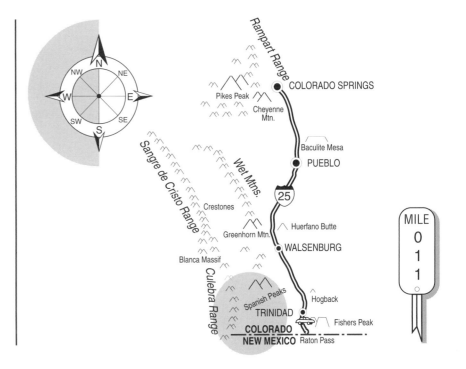

This picture, overlooking the small town of Trinidad, is taken from exit 13A. The view is north-northwest. Simpsons Rest is only 1.5 miles (2.5 km) away.

**Prospect Point** – Approx. 6,400 ft (1,951 m). A prominent sandstone cliff in the town of Trinidad.

**Simpsons Rest** – 6,420 ft (1,957 m). This sandstone cliff is named for George S. Simpson (1818–1885), an early pioneer and settler in the town of Trinidad. When a band of Ute Indians attacked Trinidad, Simpson climbed the bluff and diverted the Indians, saving the small community. At his request, Simpson is buried in a tomb on top of the bluff. A short but rough road leads to the top, providing a spectacular view south to Fishers Peak and the Raton Mesa.

George Simpson is credited with one of the first discoveries of gold along Cherry Creek, which started the famous "Pikes Peak or bust" gold rush in April 1859. He also was a founder of the Fort Pueblo trading post, located on the Arkansas River.

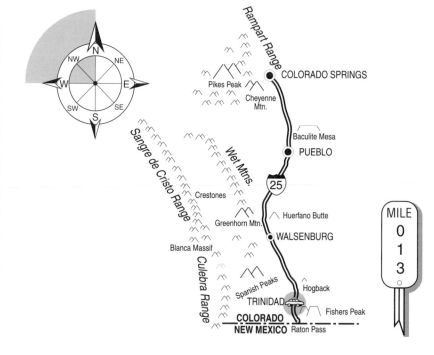

This picture looks south-southeast from the El Moro exit at mile marker 18. Fishers Peak is 9 miles (14.5 km) to the south.

**Horseshoe Mesa** – 8,802 ft (2,683 m).

**Barela Mesa** – 8,720 ft (2,658 m). Named for Senator Casimiro Barela (1847-1920), a notable resident of Trinidad in the late 1800s.

**Raton Mesa** – 9,064 ft (2,276 m). The Spanish named Raton Peak and the surrounding mesa for a small mouselike rodent that inhabits the area. *Raton* is Spanish for "mouse" or "small rodent."

**Fishers Peak Mes**a – 9,625 ft (2,934 m).

**Fishers Peak** – 9,627 ft (2,934 m). This lava-capped plateau is a prominent southern Colorado landmark. Early designations for this flat-topped mountain were Raton Peak or Cimarron Peak, as well as an old Indian name—*Chuquiriue*. Historical documents seem to place the original Fishers Peak on the mesa south of the current peak, or near the summit of Raton Pass. This *other* peak was named after Captain Waldemar Fischer, who became lost on his line of march over Raton Pass during the Mexican conflict of 1846. Fischer wanted to climb to a high point to appraise the surrounding area and regain his bearings. Years later, suspicious land dealings may have resulted in the name Fishers Peak moving to its present northerly location. By 1870, Fishers Peak had come into common use as the name for a mountain the captain apparently never climbed.

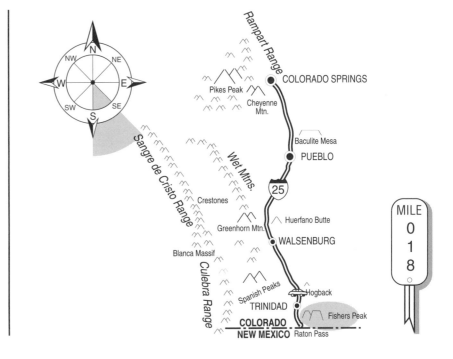

Chapter 3 • Southern I-25: New Mexico to Colorado Springs

The Hogback

This picture looks northeast from exit 30. The barren eastern plains stretch to the horizon, broken only by the lone Hogback, 6 miles (9.5 km) in the distance.

**The Hogback** – 6,584 ft (2,007 m). A hogback is a geological feature that is formed when the caprock tilts at a steep angle to the underlying bedrock. More than a dozen formations in Colorado are called the Hogback.

Bedrock is the underlying ,unweathered rock beneath the surface soil. Bedrock consists of layers of rock called beddings that have been laid down over the eons. The caprock is a hard rock that is more resistant to erosion than the softer rock below it. This can sometimes lead to different rates of erosion, 0which create many of the buttes and mesas we see today.

Tilting of the layers of bedrock happens over the millennia. Different pressures within the earth cause the bedrock layers to buckle, fracture, and split. Sometime they rise up to tremendous heights, creating hills or mountains.

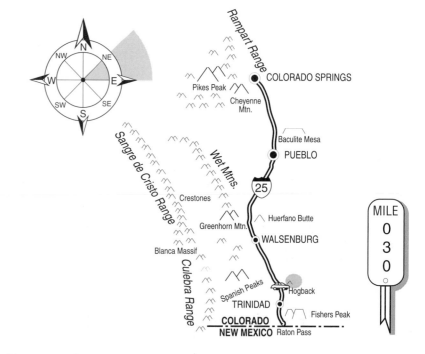

Chapter 3 • Southern I-25: New Mexico to Colorado Springs

This small rock is directly west of the I-25 southbound rest stop, at mile marker 37.

**Rugby Rock** – Approx. 6,803 ft (2,074 m). This small rock is named for the nearby town of Rugby. The town, in turn, was named by a lonely Englishman for his far-away home in Rugby, England.

**What's in a name?** – Many geological and geographical features have been named. Maybe twice as many have not. Who decides? Early settlers, explorers, and map makers named the majority of geographic features. For example, the Cache La Poudre River in northern Colorado was named because two French fur trappers stashed a supply of gunpowder for their flintlocks near the river. Common usage can sometimes override the original name, resulting in a new name or multiple names for the same feature. Legislative bodies also have changed the name of a mountain, or "moved" the name to a different summit.

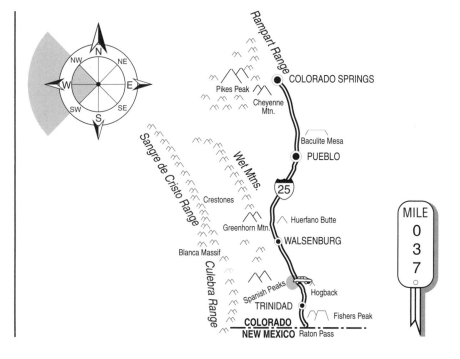

This page shows a panoramic view from exit 42 south of Walsenburg. The view is from the southwest to the northwest. The Spanish Peaks are about 19 miles (30.5 km) southwest. The Blanca Massif is 42 miles (68 km) in the distance.

**West Spanish Peak** – 13,626 ft (4,153 m). Native Americans called the Spanish Peaks *Huajatolla*, meaning "two breasts." The Spanish called them *Huatolla*, the Spanish spelling of the old Comanche word. Early settlers just called them *Las Cumbres Espanolas*— "the Spanish Peaks."

**East Spanish Peak** – 12,683 ft (3,866 m). Throughout history, many names and variant spellings have been associated with these conspicuous southern Colorado peaks. The names and spellings include *Wa-ha-toy-ah*, *Wah-to-yah*, *Wajatoya*, *Huajatolla*, *Las Cumbres Espanolas*, *Los Dos Hermanos*, and *Guajatoyan*.

**Blanca Massif** –14,345 ft (4,372 m). *Massif* is a French word for "massive." This term is often used by mountaineers to describe a cluster of mountains that rise above the surrounding low-lying ground. The Blanca Massif contains a number of peaks and can be seen for many miles.

**Mount Mestas** – 11,569 ft (3,526 m). The name of this mountain was changed in 1949 to honor Felix B. Mestas Jr. (1921-1944), who was killed during World War II in Battaqua, Italy. A total of 63 Huerfano County men died in the Second World War.

**Rough Mountain** – 11,138 ft (3,395 m).

**Silver Mountain** – 10,522 ft (3,207 m). Also known as Dike Mountain.

**Sheep Mountain** – 10,635 ft (3,242 m). A common name for Colorado mountains— there are 39 Sheep Mountains in the state. They are named for the bighorn sheep that once roamed the mountain sides in far greater numbers then they do now.

**Bighorn Sheep** – The bighorn is a remarkable animal. Its agility on rocky slopes and cliffs is due to cloven hooves with a soft cushioned sole, which aids in balance. Bighorns have acute senses of smell and hearing, along with very sharp eyesight. During mating season, the rams butt heads at speeds up to 40 miles per hour. Their clashing horns can be heard up to a mile away!

Distances to the mountains are: Mount Mestas, 23 miles (42 km); Silver Mountain, 23 miles (37 km); Sheep Mountain, 30 miles (48 km); Mount Seven, 40 miles (64 km); Greenhorn Mountain, 30 miles (48 km).

**Mount Seven** – 13,350 ft (4,069 m). From mile marker 42, this large massif just peeks above the horizon.

**Greenhorn Mountain** – 12,347 ft (3,763 m). This mountain bears the English name for the infamous Comanche chief Cuerno Verde, who was killed in a bloody battle at the foot of the peak by Governor Juan Bautista de Anza on September 3, 1779.

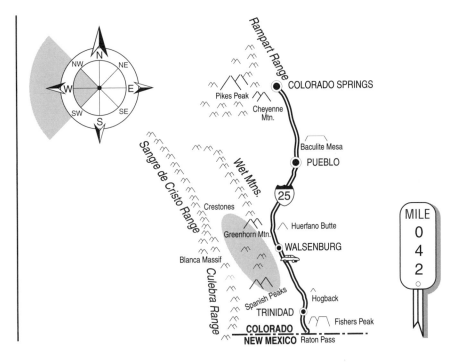

This page shows a close-up view from exit 42, south of Walsenburg. The view is west-northwest, from the Blanca Massif to the mountains northeast of there. The Blanca Massif is 42 miles (68 km) in the distance. The closer mountains, such as Silver and Mestas, are 23 miles (37 km) west.

**Hamilton Peak** – 13,658 ft (4,163 m).

**Little Bear Peak** – 14,037 ft (4,278 m).

**Blanca Peak** – 14,345 ft (4,372 m). Other names for this peak include Mount Blanca, Sierra Blanca Peak, and Sierra Blanco.

**Mount Lindsey** – 14,042 ft (4,280 m). Formerly known as Old Baldy Peak.

**Unnamed** – 13,828 ft (4,215 m).

**Mount Mestas** – 11,569 ft (3,526 m). Named for Felix B. Mestas Jr. (1921-1944). While retreating from a heavy German offensive, carrying a tripod-mounted machine gun Rambo-style on his hip to guard his comrades, Mestas took the lives of 26 enemy soldiers before he died. Mestas earned the nickname "cowboy" for his shooting-from-the-hip style.

**Rough Mountain** – 11,138 ft (3,395 m).

**Iron Mountain** – 11,411 ft (3,478 m). According to Robert Ormes, a great Colorado mountaineer, the old-time Spanish-speaking locals called this mountain *Palo Duro*, which means "hard stick," for the prickly, tough brush that grows in the vicinity.

**Silver Mountain** – 10,522 ft (3,207 m). Also known as Dike Mountain.

**Sheep Mountain** – 10,635 ft (3,242 m). This was once the home of Rocky Mountain bighorn sheep, whose numbers have been greatly reduced by hunting and encroachment by civilization on their lands.

**Mount Seven** – 13,350 ft (4,069 m). The seven distinct peaks on this massif have never been officially named. Bob Ormes, noted Colorado author and mountaineer, reported that three of the subpeaks were named XL Mountain (for a cattle brand), Medano Peak, and Hudson Branch Peak (for a creek flowing east off the peak). These names have never been recognized by the U.S. Board on Geographic Names.

MILE
0
4
2

*See map on page 35.*

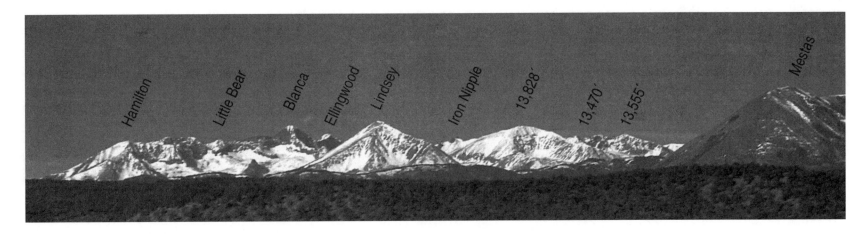

This picture is an extreme close-up of the Blanca Massif from mile marker 42, looking west-northwest. The Blanca Massif is the southern most portion of the Sangre de Cristo mountains. The peaks are about 42 miles (68 km) in the distance.

**Hamilton Peak** – 13,658 ft (4,163 m). Possibly named for William B. Hamilton (1845-1935). "Uncle Billy" was the first postmaster of La Veta and was once the mayor of Pueblo.

**Little Bear Peak** – 14,037 ft (4,278 m). First known as West Peak, the name was changed to Little Bear after the name of the creek nestled at the base of the mountain. Oddly enough, the name of this creek was changed to Tobin Creek in 1921.

**Blanca Peak** – 14,345 ft (4,372 m). The translation from Spanish is "White Mountain," probably because the mountain is snow-capped most of the year. This mountain has sheer rock faces, characteristic of many peaks in the Sangre de Cristo Range.

**Ellingwood Point** – 14,042 ft (4,280 m). Named in 1972 to honor Albert R. Ellingwood (1888-1934). Ellingwood was a distinguished Colorado mountaineer. Some of the first ascents he made are the South and Middle Tetons in Wyoming, Crestone Peak, Crestone Needle, Kit Carson Mountain, and numerous technical routes on other Colorado mountains.

**Mount Lindsey** – 14,042 ft (4,280 m). In 1953 the Colorado Mountain Club successfully petitioned the U.S. Board on Geographic Names to rename this peak in honor of Malcolm Lindsey (1880-1951). Lindsey was a very active member of the community and the Colorado Mountain Club.

He introduced many young people to the mountains and wilderness of Colorado. Prior to 1953, when the mountain was renamed Mount Lindsey, it was known by the unimaginative name of "Old Baldy." Baldy is a very common name for mountains extending above treeline.

**Iron Nipple** – 13,360 ft (4,072 m).

**Unnamed** – 13,828 ft (4,215 m).

**Unnamed** – 13,470 ft (4,106 m).

**Unnamed** – 13,555 ft (4,132 m).

**Mount Mestas** – 11,569 ft (3,526 m).

*See map on page 35.*

East Spanish      West Spanish

This panorama looks west from mile marker 45, just south of Walsenburg. The Spanish Peaks are 18 miles (29 km) distant.

**West Spanish Peak** – 13,626 ft (4,153 m). These striking mountains, West Spanish Peak and East Spanish Peak, are collectively referred to as the Spanish Peaks. The view of the mountains from this part of Interstate 25 is splendid.

**East Spanish Peak** – 12,683 ft (3,866 m). The Spanish Peaks were known to early Native Americans as *Huajatolla*, meaning "two breasts." Passed down by the Indians from generation to generation is this short verse: "Huajatolla are two breasts as round as woman's, and all living things on earth, mankind, beasts, and plants, derive their sustenance from that source. The clouds are born there, and without clouds there is no rain. And when no rain falls, we have no food, and without food—we must perish all."

The Native American name *Huajatolla* or "*Wah-ha-toy-ah*" is sometimes credited to an old chief who honored his favorite wife by bestowing her name on the mountains.

**Blanca Massif** – 14,345 ft (4,372 m).

**Mount Mestas** – 11,569 ft (3,526 m). Formerly known as La Veta Peak; *veta* is Spanish for "vein." Older names for the mountain included Veta Mountain and Baldy Peak.

**Castle Rocks** – 6,480 ft (1,975 m). Use your imagination to see where this name came from.

**Rough Mountain** – 11,138 ft (3,395 m).

**Silver Mountain** – 10,522 ft (3,207 m).

**Sheep Mountain** – 10,635 ft (3,242 m).

Oddly enough, the fairly large bluff west of the interstate has no name.

The Blanca Massif is 40 miles (64 km) to the west. Castle Rocks are 1.5 miles (2.5 km), Point of Rocks are 33 miles (53 km), Carbonate Mountain is 43 miles (69 km), and Mount Seven is about 46 miles (74 km) in the distance.

**Carbonate Mountain** – 12,308 ft (3,751 m). Carbonate is a gold-bearing rock that was found on this mountain.

**Point of Rocks** – 8,130 ft (2,478 m).

**Mount Seven** – 13,350 ft (4,069 m). In 1970, the U.S. Board on Geographic Names officially named Mount Seven for the seven distinct peaks on this massif. The name was changed from Mount Seven to Mount Herard in 1984, but the old name still seems to be the most popular. This mountain has also been known as Mount Cleveland and Medano Peak.

Through the years, stories of gold and lost riches have circulated about the Spanish Peaks. Although no gold has ever been found near the mountains, golden riches can be seen in the beautiful autumn views of these stately peaks.

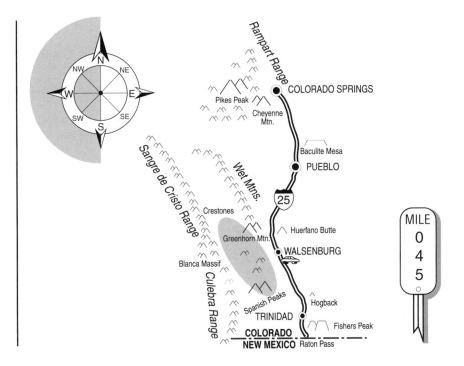

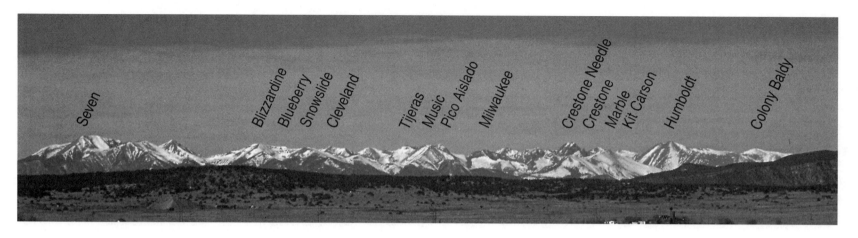

Looking northwest, this close-up shows the towering summits of the Sangre de Cristo Range. The peaks are about 45 miles (72 km) distant. Sangre de Cristo means "blood of christ" and comes from the early Spanish explorer Valverde, who saw the range basked in early morning light, knelt, and said, "*sangre de Cristo.*"

**Mount Seven** – 13,350 ft (4,069 m).

**Blizzardine Peak** – 11,910 ft (3,360 m).

**Blueberry Peak** – 12,005 ft (3,605 m).

**Snowslide Mountain** – 11,664 ft (3,555 m).

**Cleveland Peak** – 13,414 ft (4,089 m). Named for a bay (reddish-brown) race horse that came to the San Luis Valley from England.

**Tijeras Peak** – 13,604 ft (4,146 m). Spanish for "scissors." This mountain takes its name from the east ridge, which forms a scissors-shape or "V" with two forks of Sand Creek.

**Music Mountain** – 13,355 ft (4,071 m). Named for the singing sounds often heard in the wind blowing across the Great Sand Dunes, several miles from the peak.

**Pico Aislado** – 13,611 ft (4,419 m). This means "Isolated Peak" in Spanish—no doubt for its remote location.

**Milwaukee Peak** – 13,522 ft (4,122 m). An older name for this peak is Cold Peak, suggestive of the temperatures high in the Sangre de Cristo mountains.

**Crestone Needle** – 14,197 ft (4,327 m). The summits of Crestone Needle and Crestone Peak are only about half a mile apart. Their tops look like a cockscomb, and *crestone*, is a derivative word from the Spanish *cresta*, meaning "crest," and *creton* for "cockscomb."

**Crestone Peak** – 14,294 ft (4,357 m). Crestone Peak and Needle, together with their neighbor, Kit Carson Mountain, originally were called the Three Tetons, or *Trois Tetons*, for their resemblance to the Teton Mountains of Wyoming.

**Marble Mountain** – 13,266 ft (4,043 m). Near this mountain is Marble Cave, which in the past has been called the Cave of Gold. Legends of gold and silver in this cave have persisted throughout Colorado history, however, none has ever been found.

**Kit Carson Mountain** – 14,165 ft (4,317 m). This peak's name honors the great frontiersman and soldier Kit Carson (1809–1868). It's rumored that Carson spent time in a cabin near the mountain.

**Humboldt Peak** – 14,064 ft (4,287 m). Named for Alexander von Humboldt (1769–1859), a German geographer, explorer, and mountaineer.

**Colony Baldy** – 13,705 ft (4,177 m). The unimaginative name Baldy Peak was once bestowed upon this mountain. Since 1970 the name officially has been Colony Baldy, after Colony Creek, which flows beneath the mountain. The Colony Creeks are, in turn, named after the early immigrant colonies in the Wet Mountain Valley.

This close-up from mile marker 53 looks southwest to the Culebra Range. Trinchera Peak and the Culebra Range are approximately 33 miles (53 km) to the southwest. The word *Culebra* appears on maps dated to 1810.

**Mariquita Peak** – 13,405 ft (4,086 m).

**Mount Maxwell** – 13,335 ft (4,065 m).

**Cuatro Peak** – 13,487 ft (4,111 m).

**Trinchera Peak** – 13,517 ft (4,120 m). Franklin Rhoda, a great topographer with the Hayden Survey, along with Frederick Endlich, climbed this peak on September 27, 1875. While in deep snow at about 13,000 feet, they found fresh tracks of a grizzly bear, which they followed like stepping stones to the summit.

**Unnamed** – 12,930 ft. (3,941 m).

**Unnamed** – 12,630 ft. (3,850 m).

**Teddys Peak** – 12,402 ft (3,780 m). This mountain is named for Theodore Roosevelt (1882-1945), the 26th president of the United States, who hunted in this area of southern Colorado.

**Park Mountain** – 11,670 ft (3,557 m).

**Napoleon Peak** – 11,866 ft (3,617 m). Speculation has it that this mountain is named for Napoleon Bonaparte, but this has never been substantiated.

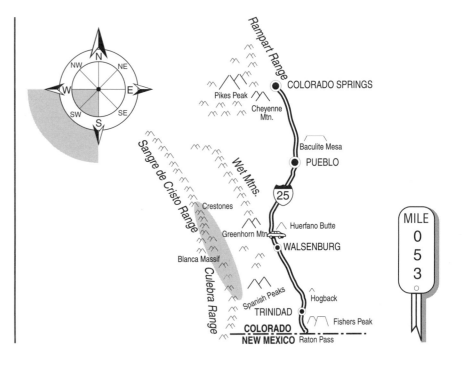

From mile marker 53, just north of Walsenburg looking west, Mestas, Sheep, and Little Sheep are all 21 miles (34 km) to the west. Silver Mountain is 17 miles (27 km) away, Iron is 26 miles (42 km) away, and California Peak is 39 miles (62 km) in the distance. At the foot of Sheep Mountain are the Black Hills, 9 miles (15 km) away.

**Mount Mestas** – 11,569 ft (3,526 m). At the bottom of La Veta Pass is a monument to Felix B. Mestas Jr. and the 62 other Huerfano County men who lost their lives in World War II.

**Silver Mountain** – 10,522 ft (3,207 m).

**Iron Mountain** – 11,411 ft (3,478 m). Early settlers probably named this peak for the iron ore that can be seen in the rock.

**Unnamed** – 13,828 ft. (4,215 m).

**Sheep Mountain** – 10,635 ft (3,242 m).

**Little Sheep Mountain** – 9,610 ft (2,929 m).

**Black Hills** – 7,516 ft (2,291 m). The Black Hills are composed of soft rock encased by magma. Many of the geological features in southern Colorado are a result of volcanic activity millions of years ago.

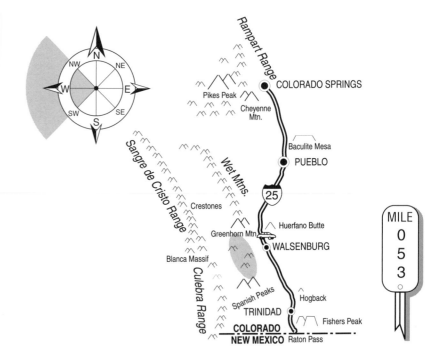

This view, looking to the northwest, is from mile marker 54. Greenhorn Mountain and Badito Cone are about 18 miles (29 km) and 14 miles (23 km) away, respectively. Farther west, the massive Sangre de Cristo Range can be seen at 42 miles (68 km). Some of the remote roads and trails in the Sangres are clear of snow only from late June through mid-September.

**Sangre de Cristo Range** – The highest point in this range is Blanca Peak, 14,345 ft (4,372 m). The "Sangres," which extend into New Mexico, are the longest continuous mountain range in the Rocky Mountains—more than 230 miles (370 km) long. The width of the range is about 20 miles (32 km).

On the west side of the Sangre de Cristos lies a sea of sand—the Great Sand Dunes National Monument. These dunes, stretching more than 50 square miles (80 square km), were created over eons of time by ever-blowing winds. The sand is piled more than 700 ft (215 m) high, making these the tallest sand dunes in the United States.

**Badito Cone** – 8,942 ft (2,726 m). Named for a settlement near a crossing of the Huerfano River, along the Sangre de Cristo Trail. This trail was used by early trappers.

**Greenhorn Mountain** – 12,347 ft (3,763 m). Named for the Comanche Chief Cuerno Verde. Cuerno Verde received his name from tribal elders, because of his fearless and cocky behavior, characteristic of a young buck whose antlers are still green. Today, "greenhorn" has come to mean an inexperienced or immature person.

**North Peak** – 12,220 ft (3,725 m). A nearby neighbor to Greenhorn Mountain. The two summits are 1.75 miles (2.8 km) apart.

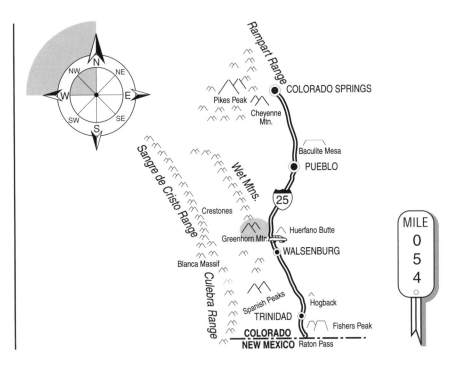

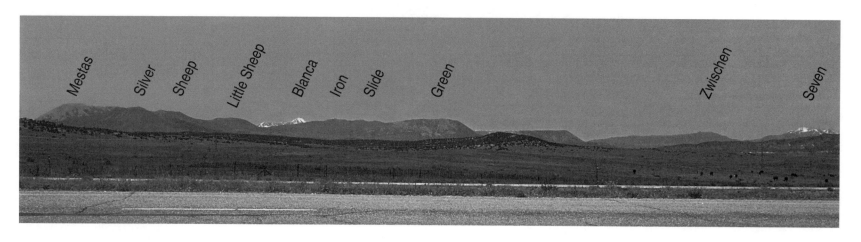

From mile marker 56, looking west, Slide and Green mountains are about 25 miles (40 km) in the distance. Mount Zwischen and Mount Seven are about 37 miles (60 km) west.

**Mount Mestas** – 11,569 ft (3,526 m).

**Silver Mountain** – 10,522 ft (3,207 m).

**Little Sheep Mountain** – 9,610 ft (2,929 m).

**Sheep Mountain** – 10,635 ft (3,242 m).

**Blanca Peak** – 14,345 ft (4,372 m).

**Iron Mountain** – 11,411 ft (3,478 m).

**Slide Mountain** – 12,306 ft (3,751 m).

**Green Mountain** – 11,400 ft (3,475 m).

**Mount Zwischen** – 12,006 ft (3,659 m). Named for an early German settlement in the Wet Mountain Valley. The German word *zwischen* means "between."

**Mount Seven** – 13,350 ft (4,069 m).

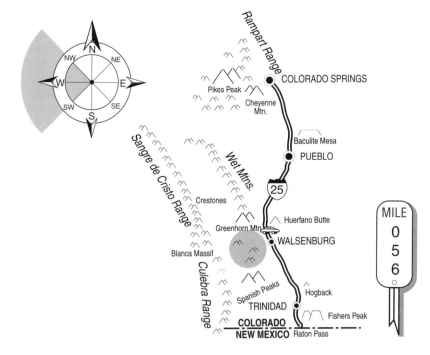

Chapter 3 • Southern I-25: New Mexico to Colorado Springs

Huerfano Butte

This volcanic remnant is located just east of Interstate 25, at mile marker 59. A scenic area to the east of the interstate provides a fine pullout for viewing. The butte is .5 miles (.8 km) west.

**Huerfano Butt**e – 6,166 ft (1,879 m). Spanish records as early as 1818 refer to this dark volcanic cone as *el Huerfano*, which means "the Orphan." This lonely landmark, sometimes called the "Lone Rock of the Huerfano," rises 370 feet above the plains. In very early writings, the landmark is referred to as Wafno, Harfno, and Wolfano. Several important early trails and water routes pass within sight of this ancient guidepost, including the Taos Trail and the Santa Fe Trail. Native Americans, Spaniards, trappers, and early Colorado settlers used the dark landmark as a reference point. However, no settlements were founded in this dry and barren land. Settlers preferred the wetter lands to the north, around Greenhorn Peak.

This small cone, a remnant of volcanic activity, is approximately 30 million years old—just a couple of ticks of the geological clock.

In 1847, Senator Thomas Hart Benton of Missouri, a strong proponent of a centrally located railroad to the Pacific Ocean, suggested in his first Senate speech placing a colossal statue of John C. Frémont—the great explorer of the American West—atop Huerfano Butte. Thomas Hart Benton was Frémont's father-in-law. A variant of this story says the good Senator suggested placing a statue of Cristopher Columbus atop the isolated butte.

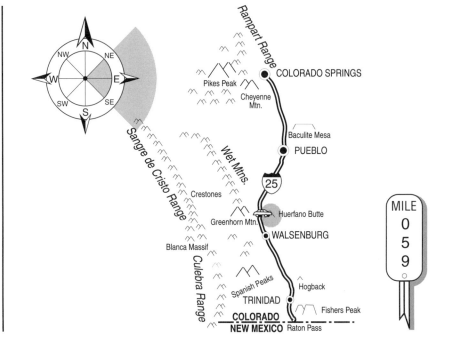

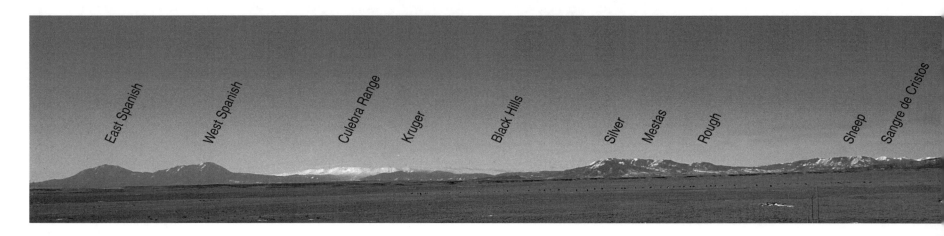

From Lascar Road, mile marker 64, this panoramic view looks from the south-southwest to the west. The towering Spanish Peaks can be seen 32 miles to the south. The Culebra Range is approximately 45 miles away. The southern tip of the Sangre de Cristo Range can be seen 18 miles (29 km) away. Silver, Mestas, Rough, and Sheep are about 23 miles (37 km) away.

**East Spanish Peak** – 12,683 ft (3,866 m).

**West Spanish Peak** – 13,626 ft (4,153 m). The Spanish Peaks, which are not part of the Culebra Range, are formed of igneous rock. Surrounding the mountains, like spokes on a wheel, are rock dikes spawned from molten magma. These dikes have eroded over the centuries, but they can still be seen stretching out in almost all directions around the two peaks.

**Culebra Range** – The Culebra Range is sometimes considered an extension of the Sangre de Cristo Range, although technically they are distinct and independent ranges.

The Culebra Range is crossed or bounded by eight mountain passes. They are North La Veta Pass, La Veta Pass, Veta Pass, Pass Creek Pass, Cucharas Pass, Cordova Pass, Whiskey Pass, and San Francisco Pass. No paved road crosses directly over the Culebra Range. Whiskey Pass, located between the summits of Beaubien Peak and De Anza Peak (see panorama at mile marker 11), crosses the snowy summits but is just a dirt trail.

**Kruger Mountain** – 9,488 ft (2,895 m). Most likely named after a person whose identity has been lost to history.

**Black Hills** – 7,516 ft (2,291 m).

The Culebra Range has 17 officially named peaks: Beaubien Peak, Cuatro Peak, Culebra Peak, De Anza Peak, Francisco Peak, Lomo Liso Mountain, Mariquita Peak, Miranda Peak, Mount Maxwell, Napoleon Peak, Park Mountain, Purgatoire Peak, Red Mountain, State Line Peak, Teddys Peak, Trinchera Peak, and Vermejo Peak. Two peaks have unofficial names, Leaning South Peak and Leaning North Peak (located south of Trinchera Peak), and two are unnamed summits, 12,930 feet and 12,630 feet high.

**Silver Mountain** – 10,522 ft (3,207 m).

**Mount Mestas** – 11,569 ft (3,526 m).

**Rough Mountain** – 11,138 ft (3,395 m). Although it appears that Silver Mountain, Mount Mestas, and Rough Mountain are not part of the Culebra Range, technically they are. The Culebras' northern end is Sangre de Cristo Pass, which is just to the north of Rough Mountain.

**Sheep Mountain** – 10,635 ft (3,242 m).

Badito Cone and Greenhorn Peak lie 8 miles (13 km) to the west. Both peaks are at the southern end of the Wet Mountains. This range also was known as the Greenhorn Range because Greenhorn mountain is its predominant peak.

**Sangre de Cristo Range** – Some of the mountains in the Sangres, as the locals call them, were among the last summits in Colorado to be explored and climbed. Albert Ellingwood led climbs of the 14,000-foot peaks in this range in 1916. These rugged mountains contain more than 350 square miles (915 square km) of designated wilderness area.

Wilderness areas are lands that have been relatively undisturbed by mankind, set aside by Congress in the hopes of maintaining and preserving their ecosystems. No vehicles are allowed. Development, logging, or mining are prohibited. Man is just a visitor to these areas.

A hiking or backpacking trip into the Sangre de Cristo mountains is a wonderful scenic adventure. Filled with lakes, alpine tarns, and waterfalls nestled below towering peaks, the Sangres offer magnificent scenery.

**Badito Cone** – 8,942 ft (2,726 m). Most likely named for an early settlement on the Huerfano River. *Badito* translates loosely as "the place where the river was forded."

**Greenhorn Mountain** – 12,347 ft (3,763 m).

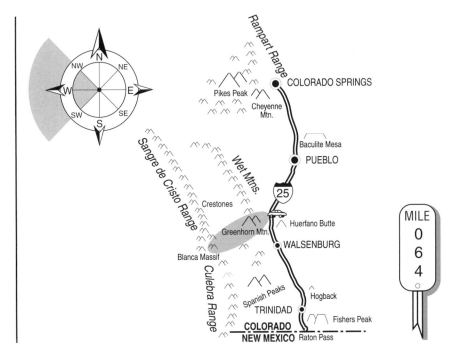

This picture looks southwest from exit 83, 12 miles south of Pueblo. Far to the south, the Spanish Peaks can be seen 50 miles (80 km) away. The 30-mile-long Culebra Range can be seen at a distance of about 64 miles (103 km). Silver Mountain and Mount Mestas peek above the horizon 41 miles (67 km) away. Greenhorn and North are at 21 miles (34 km).

**East Spanish Peak** – 12,683 ft (3,866 m). The summits of East and West Spanish Peaks are about 3 miles (4.8 km) apart.

**West Spanish Peak** – 13,626 ft (4,153 m). The Spanish Peaks can be seen from as far north as Colorado Springs and from far east on the plains. These mountains have been guideposts for centuries to Native Americans, Spanish explorers, and early settlers.

**Culebra Range** – The highest point in this range is Culebra Peak, 14,047 ft (4,282 m). The range runs approximately 30 miles, from Sangre de Cristo Pass on the north to Costilla and Comanche Creeks on the south.

**Silver Mountain** – 10,522 ft (3,207 m).

**Mount Mestas** – 11,569 ft (3,526 m).

**Greenhorn Mountain** – 12,347 ft (3,763 m).

**North Peak** – 12,220 ft (3,725 m).

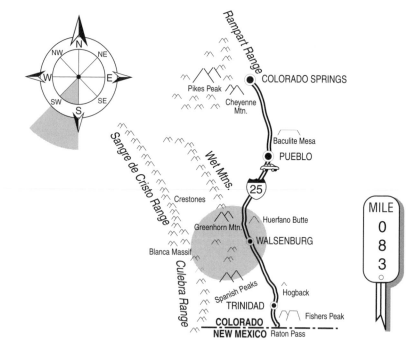

This picture looks southwest to the Wet Mountains from exit 83, approximately 12 miles south of Pueblo. The Wet Mountain Range is about 50 miles (80 km) long. It runs from here northwest to Cañon City. St. Charles Peak is 22 miles (35 km) away. Rudolph Mountain is 24 miles (39 km) away.

**Greenhorn Mountain** – 12,347 ft (3,763 m).

**North Peak** – 12,220 ft (3,725 m).

**St. Charles Peak** – 11,784 ft (3,592 m). This is most likely named for the St. Charles River.

**Scraggy Peaks** – 9,198 ft (2,804 m).

**Sperry Mountain** – 10,935 ft (3,333 m).

**Rudolph Mountain** – 10,334 ft (3,150 m).

**Wet Mountains** – 12,347 ft (3,763 m). The Wet Mountain Range is approximately 50 miles (80 km) long, stretching from northwest of Cañon City to south of Badito Cone. The words Wet Mountains are from the Spanish *Sierra Mojado,* which describe the far more abundant water in this region compared with the arid land farther south.

The Wet Mountains were once known as the Greenhorns or *Cuernos Verdes* after Greenhorn Mountain, the predominant peak in the range.

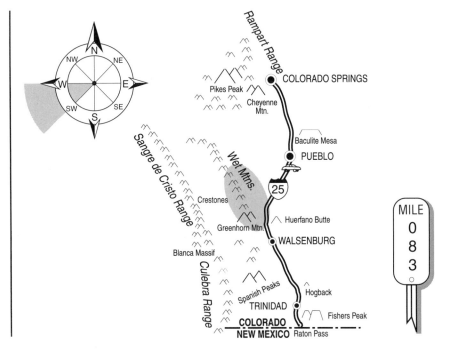

Looking southwest to the Wet Mountains from Piñon at exit 108. Distances are: Greenhorn Mountain, 44 miles (71 km); St. Charles Peak, 38 miles (62 km); and Stull Mountain, 33 miles (54 km). The tops of the Sangre de Cristo mountains can be seen behind the Wet Mountains. The Sangres are more than 60 miles (97 km) west.

**Greenhorn Mountain** – 12,347 ft (3,763 m).

**St. Charles Peak** – 11,784 ft (3,592 m).

**Scraggy Peaks** – 9,198 ft (2,804 m). Named for their rough outline.

**Sperry Mountain** – 10,935 ft (3,333 m).

**Rudolph Mountain** – 10,334 ft (3,150 m).

**Stull Mountain** – Approx. 10,000 ft (3,048 m) This mountain is possibly named for a mining device called a stull, a timber or beam used to support the roof of a mine.

The "V" or dip to the left of Stull Mountain is the location of Hardscrabble Pass and Highway 95, which winds its way across the Wet Mountains eastward to Westcliffe.

Between Pueblo and Colorado Springs, a series of low hills and berms west of the interstate keeps the motorist from seeing the shining white Sangre de Cristo Range, except for a quick peek at their tops at mile marker 123. East of the highway are some conical hills known as Teepee Buttes.

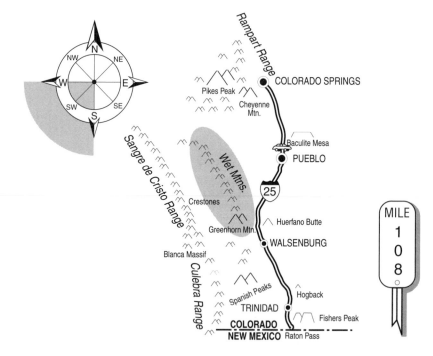

From exit 123, looking northwest to the mountains just south of Colorado Springs, the summit of Pikes Peak can just be seen above the smaller mountains, 25 miles (40 km) away. Other distances are: Cooper Mountain, 28 miles (45 km); Crown Point, 18 miles (29 km); and Cheyenne Mountain, 14 miles (23 km).

**Cooper Mountain** – 9,146 ft (2,788 m).

**Sugar Loaf** – 7,456 ft (2,273 m). The name comes from early settlers, who bought their raw sugar in hard, conical loaves. No doubt, sweet-toothed pioneers saw "sugar loaves" among the many mountain peaks.

**Crown Point** – 11,463 ft (3,494 m).

**Black Mountain** – 10,132 ft (3,088 m).

**Sheep Mountain** – 12,397 ft (3,779 m). A common mountain name.

**Mount Rosa** – 11,499 ft (3,505 m). Robert Ormes (1904-1994), noted Colorado author and mountaineer, stated that both times he had climbed this peak, he found the summit covered in lady bugs.

**Pikes Peak** – 14,110 ft (4,301 m). Katherine Lee Bates, author of *America the Beautiful*, wrote her famous song inspired by views from the top of this mountain.

**Cheyenne Mountain** – 9,565 ft (2,915 m). Nestled at the base of this mountain is the city of Colorado Springs.

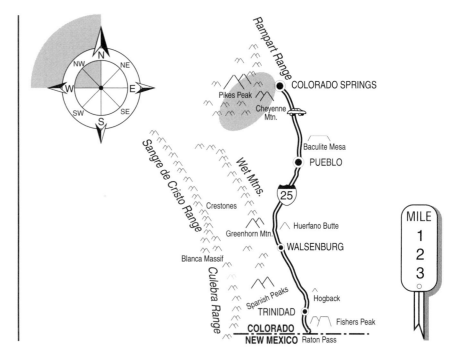

# Central I-25: Colorado Springs to Denver

## TRIP HIGHLIGHTS

- Marvelous views of the Continental Divide.

- Panoramic vistas and rugged buttes.

- Majestic Pikes Peak.

Castle Rock

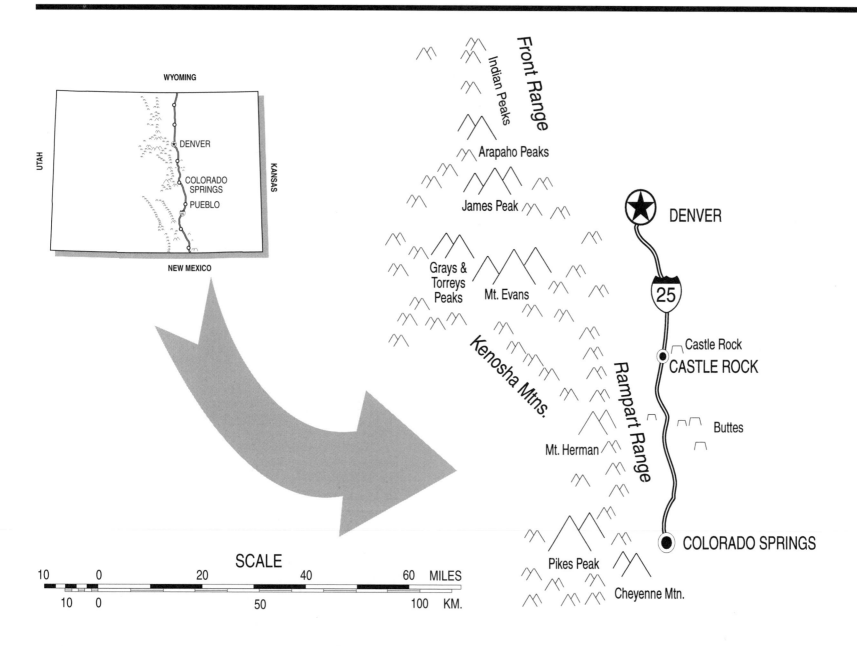

Map of central I-25 from Colorado Springs to Denver

This is the southern tip of the Colorado Front Range. Nestled at the base are the cities of Manitou Springs and Colorado Springs. Most of the rock here is pink granite. Behind these mountains only 17 miles (27 km) as the crow flies are the towns of Cripple Creek and Victor, where the largest gold deposit in the world was found. Pikes Peak is obscured by the smaller hills in this picture.

**Cheyenne Mountain** – 9,565 ft (2,915 m). This hard-granite mountain is home to the North American Aerospace Defense Command (NORAD). Often called the Cheyenne Mountain Complex, NORAD is buried deep within the mountain.

**The Horns** – 9,212 ft (2,808 m). These craggy rocks look just like horns. A local legend says that an Indian god battled and defeated a devil, then buried him atop Cheyenne Mountain up to his horns.

**Gray Back Peak** – 9,348 ft (2,849 m).

**Mount Vigil** – 10,073 ft (3,070 m). Named for Cornelio Vigil, who, together with Ceran St. Vrain, received from the Mexican government four million acres in southern Colorado, the largest land grant in Colorado history.

**St. Peters Dome** – 9,665 ft (2,946 m). Richard M. Pearl in his book *Colorado Gem Trails and Mineral Guide*, calls the St. Peters Dome area "one of the outstanding mineral localities of the world. Noted for its many rare species and good quality of some of its more common (minerals)." Smoky quartz, zircon, topaz, and cryolite are just a few of the minerals that can be found in the area.

*(Continued on next page)*

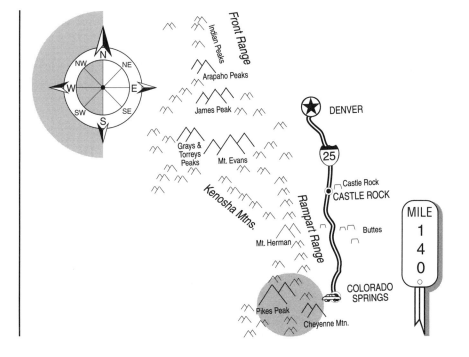

*(Continued from last page)*

**Stove Mountain** – 9,782 ft (2,982 m). This rocky, flat-topped peak has also been known as Cook Stove Mountain, for its stove-top appearance.

**Mount Rosa** – 11,499 ft (3,505 m). Named for Rose Kingsley (1845-?), the daughter of English author and clergyman Charles Kingsley (1819-1875). Rose spent time visiting and writing about Colorado Springs during the city's very early days.

**Kineo Mountain** – 9,478 ft (2,889 m).

**Almagre Mountain** – 12,367 ft (3,769 m). This mountain is named for the red color of the granite found in the Pikes Peak area. *Almagre* is an old Spanish word which roughly translates as "red ocher."

**Mount Garfield** – Approx. 10,900 ft (3,322 m). Named in honor of President James A. Garfield (1831-1881), who was assassinated shortly after taking office. At least six Colorado geographic features are named after the 20th president.

**Mount Arthur** – 10,807 ft (3,294 m). Named for the 21st president of the United States, Chester A. Arthur (1830-1886), who assumed the office after Garfield's assassination.

**Tenney Crags** – 10,094 ft (3,077 m). This pillar is named for the first president of Colorado College, Edward Tenney (1835-1916). These crags have also been called Specimen Rocks and Sentinel Rock.

**Cameron Cone** – 10,707 ft (3,263 m). General R. A. Cameron (1828-1894), founder of the town of Greeley, has his name bestowed on a mountain and a pass, but this mountain is named after another Cameron whose identity is lost. The summit is sometimes called Camerons Cone.

*See map on previous page.*

MILE
1
4
0

This picture looks west from the scenic pullout (southbound I-25 only) at mile marker 152. Cheyenne Mountain and Pikes Peak are almost 16 miles away. Pikes Peak has the greatest base-to-summit relief of any Colorado mountain — 8,000 feet (2,440 m). The reddish scars below and to the right of Pikes Peak are from rock quarries. Extensive reclamation and reseeding shows as a green tint on the slopes in the summertime.

**Cheyenne Mountain** – 9,565 ft (2,915 m).

**Stove Mountain** – 9,782 ft (2,982 m).

**Mount Rosa** – 11,499 ft (3,505 m).

**Almagre Mountain** – 12,367 ft (3,769 m).

**Sachett Mountain** – 12,560 ft (3,828 m). Named for David H. Sackett, the energetic sergeant who lived and worked in the old weather station at the summit of Pikes Peak during the early 1870s.

**Pikes Peak** – 14,110 ft (4,301 m). The Pikes Peak Toll Road, a cog railway, and the long and steep Barr Trail lead visitors to the top of the mountain, providing spectacular views in all directions.

**Ormes Peak** – 9,727 ft (2,965 m). Named for Manly D. Ormes (1858-1929).

**Blodgett Peak** – 9,423 ft (2,872 m).

**North Peak** – 9,368 ft (2,855 m).

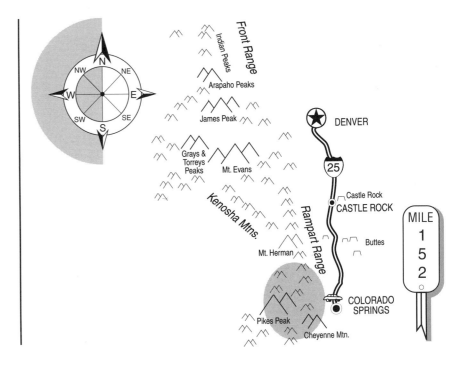

This is a two-page panorama looking west from mile marker 158. These mountains are part of the Rampart Range, a subrange of the Front Range.

**Cheyenne Mountain** – 9,565 ft (2,915 m). It is a common misconception that the antennas atop Cheyenne mountain belong to NORAD. The antennas actually belong to various radio and television stations in the region.

**Mount Rosa** – 11,499 ft (3,505 m).

**Almagre Mountain** – 12,367 ft (3,769 m). The summit ridge of this mountain is almost three miles long.

**Blodgett Peak** – 9,423 ft (2,872 m). This mountain may be named after a rancher by the name of Blodgett, who lived at the base of this mountain.

**Pikes Peak** – 14,110 ft (4,301 m). The saying "Pikes Peak or bust" became a household phrase after the April 1858 gold rush, when gold was discovered along Cherry Creek, farther north in Colorado. This mountain often was the first peak seen as miners rushed westward across the plains in search of their fortunes.

**Monument** – The town of Monument is named for the white sandstone columns west of the town and north of Mount Herman.

**Ormes Peak** – 9,727 ft (2,965 m). Manly D. Ormes was a resident of Colorado Springs and librarian at Colorado College. Ormes also was a prominent Colorado mountaineer. Ormes' son Robert (1904-1994) grew up to be an English professor at Colorado College, and was also a noted author, climber, and lover of the mountains. He spent his life exploring and writing about the Colorado high country. Robert Ormes christened the mountain for his father on July 23, 1933, on the summit itself. Before the name change, the mountain was known as Red Mountain.

It is hoped that with the passing of Robert Ormes, a suitable mountain, perhaps within eyesight of the mountain honoring his father, will one day be renamed for the younger Ormes by the U.S. Board on Geographic Names.

**North Peak** – 9,368 ft (2,855 m). North and South Peaks are sometimes called the Academy Peaks for their close proximity to the U.S. Air Force Academy. If you look closely, the shiny spires of the Air Force chapel can be seen below and to the left of the mountain. North Peak has also been known as Mount Harmon, after the first superintendent of the Air Force Academy, Lt. General Hubert R. Harmon.

The bare rock of this peak reportedly provides nesting places for prairie falcons. In the past, Academy cadets would scale the mountain in search of young falcons for training.

To the north of Mount Herman is the Palmer Divide, which separates the Platte River and Arkansas River watersheds.

**South Peak** – 9,321 ft (2,855 m).

**Mount Herman** – 9,063 ft (2,762 m).

**Raspberry Mountain** – 8,634 ft (2,632 m). It is believed that this mountain is named for a prospector named Roseberry, who held a placer claim on the west side of the mountain. Unfortunately, there are no raspberries on the mountain.

**Chautauqua Mountain** – 8,352 ft (2,546 m).

**Sundance Mountain** – 8,255 ft (2,516 m).

**The Rampart Range** – The Rampart Range runs from Colorado Springs north to Castle Rock, and is about 38 miles (61 km) long. The range may get its name for its similarity to the tall, sheer walls of a castle's fortifications. The Ramparts rise abruptly from the plains more then 2,500 feet (750 m).

Pikes Peak, also a part of the Front Range, is not considered part of the Rampart Range. The large Pikes Peak Massif sits alone, marking the southern end of the great Colorado Front Range.

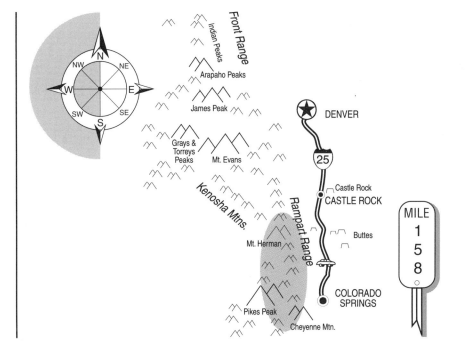

This picture looks north from the Greenland exit, at mile marker 167. On clear days, you can see the Mount Evans group, between Raspberry Butte and Dawson Butte, 50 miles (80 km) in the distance.

**Raspberry Butte** – 7,680 ft (2,341 m).

**Monkey Face** – 7,719 ft (2,353 m). From a few miles farther north, by the rest stop at mile marker 170, look west to this small butte. The eastern side looks remarkably like the face of a monkey.

**Dawson Butte** – 7,481 ft (2,280 m).

**Larkspur Butte** – 7,535 ft (2,297 m). Probably named after the beautiful wildflower that grows in Colorado.

**Rattlesnake Butte** – 7,570 ft (2,307 m). No doubt named for the deadly snakes found here and farther east on the high plains of Colorado.

**Nemrick Butte** – 7,465 ft (2,275 m).

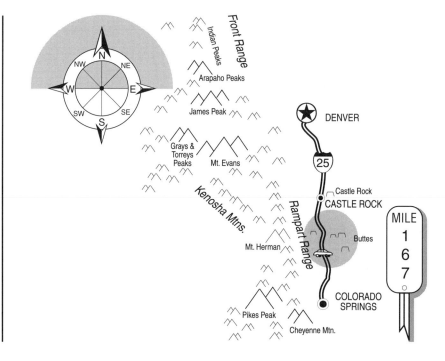

Castle Rock

This photo looks south-southeast to Castle Rock. There are 18 geographical features in Colorado named Castle Rock. During the winter holidays a large lighted star shines atop this butte, visible for many miles.

**Castle Rock** – 6,586 ft (2,007 m). The town of Castle Rock is named for this conspicuous landmark itself, named by Edwin James of the Longs expedition in 1820. James noted "its striking resemblance to a work of art. It has columns, and porticoes, and arches, and, when seen from a distance, has an astonishingly regular and artificial appearance." Early on, this prominent landmark also was known as Pound Cake Rock.

The Castle Rock rises approximately 350 feet above the surrounding valley. On the south side of the butte a trail leads to the top, providing a fine view of the Front Range to the west and the town of Castle Rock below.

**The geology of Castle Rock** – The hard-capped top of this prominent landmark is composed of sand and small pebbles cemented into a rock known as a conglomerate. Because this cap rock is very resistant to erosion, the surrounding softer rock erodes at a much faster pace. Some of the buttes south of Castle Rock, including Larkspur Butte, Dawson Butte, and Rattlesnake Butte, are also capped with hard conglomerates.

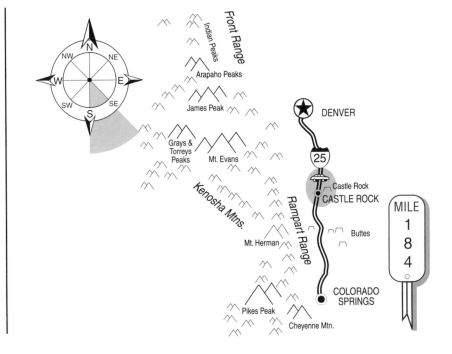

This picture looks south to Pikes Peak, 40 miles (64 km) away. The very top of Almagre Mountain is just visible above the horizon.

**Castle Rock** – 6,586 ft (2,007 m).

**Sachett Mountain** – 12,560 ft (3,828 m).

**Almagre Mountain** – 12,367 ft (3,769 m) This peak has also been known as Bald Mountain, Mount Almagre, and Sierra Almagre.

**Pikes Peak** – 14,110 ft (4,301 m). Pikes Peak was named for Lt. Zebulon Pike (1779-1813), who in 1806 became the first white American to sight it. He dubbed it Grand Peak and attempted to climb the mountain but turned back before reaching the summit. Stephan Long later named the summit James Peak, after a member of his expedition who first climbed the great mountain. Colonel Henry Dodge and John C. Frémont used the name Pikes Peak on maps in 1835 and 1843, respectively.

The Arapaho Indians, who lived farther north, called the mountain "Long Peak," for the long north ridge they saw when looking south to the great massif. The Pawnee name for Pikes Peak is *La-Wah-Oo-Kah-Tah*, "Mountain that Reaches the Sky."

**Raspberry Mountain** – 8,634 ft (2,632 m).

**Dawson Butte** – 7,481 ft (2,280 m).

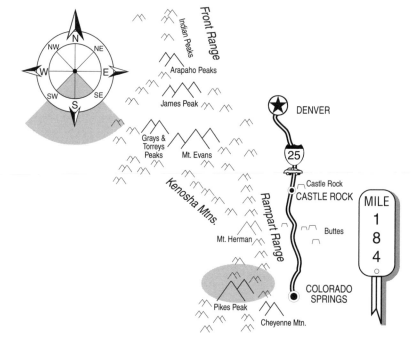

This picture is a close-up view of Pikes Peak, 40 miles (64 km) to the south-southwest. Notice the long, steep north face of the mountain.

**Almagre Mountain** – 12,367 ft (3,769 m).

**Pikes Peak** – 14,110 ft (4,301 m). Edwin James (see James Peak), a botanist with the Long expedition, made the first recorded ascent of the mountain in 1820. Major Long, the leader of the expedition, failed in his attempt to rename the peak after James.

**AdAMan** – In 1922, on New Year's Eve, five men climbed to the top of Pikes Peak. Each year since, the AdAMan Club invites one new member to make the long, cold journey to the summit of the mountain, where they stage an elaborate fireworks display.

Each summer on the Fourth of July, the famous Pikes Peak Auto Hill Climb, a race to the top of the peak, is held.

**Pikes Peak** and Mount Evans, another Front Range giant, are the only peaks above 14,000 feet with roads leading to their tops. The views from these peaks are spectacular. On a clear day, one can see to Kansas or Wyoming.

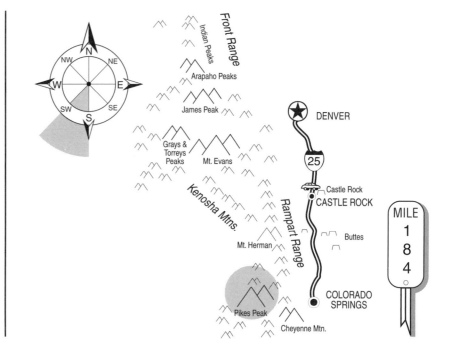

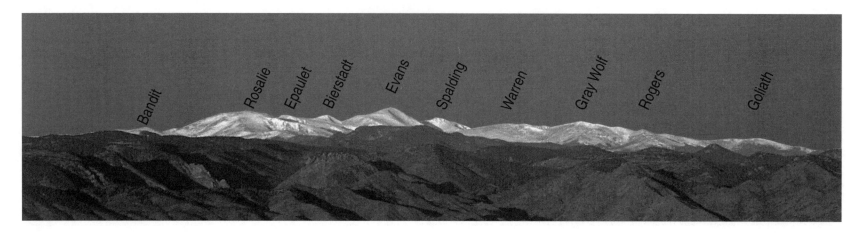

Looking to the northwest, this close-up shows the Mount Evans Group. Part of the Front Range, this cluster of mountains is 40 miles (64 km) away. Beyond them, hidden from view, is the Continental Divide, another 7 miles away.

**Bandit Peak** – 12,444 ft (3,793 m).

**Rosalie Peak** – 13,575 ft (4,138 m). Named for Rosalie Bierstadt, wife of the great, romantic, western painter Albert Bierstadt (1830-1902). Originally, Mr. Bierstadt named the highest peak in the Evans Group (now Mount Evans) after his loving wife. Later, the Colorado legislature moved the name to this peak.

**Epaulet Mountain** – 13,523 ft (4,122 m). Named by James Grafton Rogers in 1904 because the summit is on the shoulder of Mount Evans. Before this, the mountain was temporarily known as Mount Rosalie until the name was moved farther south. It was also known as Epaulet Peak.

**Mount Bierstadt** – 14,060 ft (4,285 m). Named for Albert Bierstadt (1830-1902), the famous landscape painter. Bierstadt painted many grand, panoramic views of the Rocky Mountains and climbed many of the peaks. His wife, Rosalie, also has a mountain named after her, southeast of Mount Evans.

**Mount Evans** – 14,264 ft (4,348 m). Named for John Evans (1814-1897), who founded Northwestern University at Evanston, Illinois, and was a leading principal in the con-struction of the Denver Pacific Railroad. The Mount Evans highway, the highest paved road in the world, leads to the top of this mountain, providing breathtaking views.

**Mount Spalding** – 13,842 ft (4,219 m). Named for William M. Spalding, an early settler who ranched at the base of this mountain.

**Mount Warren** – 13,307 (4,056 m).

**Gray Wolf Mountain** – 13,602 ft (4,146 m).

**Rogers Peak** – 13,391 ft (4,082 m). Named for James Grafton Rogers (1883-1971), a professor of law and an early lover of the Colorado mountains. Rogers is responsible for naming many Colorado peaks. Not only did he serve on the Colorado Geographic Board, he also was a president of the Colorado Mountain Club and the Colorado His-torical Society. He also served as mayor of Georgetown.

**Goliath Peak** – 12,216 ft (3,723 m).

Kenosha Mountains   Logan   Mount Evans Group   James Peak Group   Indian Peaks Group

This panorama looks to the northwest. All of the peaks in the picture are part of the Front Range. The Kenosha Mountains are 34 (55 km) miles west. The Evans group is 40 (64 km) miles northwest. The James group, which sits on the Continental Divide, is 55 (89 km) miles northwest. The Indian Peaks are more than 90 miles (145 km) to the north-northwest.

**Kenosha Mountains** – 12,429 ft (3,788 m). Named for the town of Kenosha, Wisconsin, by a homesick settler. *Kenosha* is an Algonquian Indian word for the pike fish.

**Mount Logan** – 12,871 ft (3,923 m).

**Mount Evans Group** – Mount Evans and the peaks surrounding it are conspicuous landmarks around Denver and the northern Front Range. This group of mountains first was called the Chicago Mountains by miners who came from that city in search of gold and silver. Mount Evans, 14,264 ft (4,348 m), is the highest point in the group.

**James Peak Group** – This group of mountains sits on the Continental Divide between Arapaho Pass and Berthoud Pass. James Peak, 13,294 ft (4,052 m), is the tallest of these mountains.

**Indian Peaks Group** – Most of the mountains in this group are named after Native American tribes. Most of these names were suggested by Ellsworth Bethel (1863-1925), a Denver high school botany teacher who saw the peaks from the windows of his classroom. The highest point in this group is North Arapaho Peak, 13,502 ft (4,115 m).

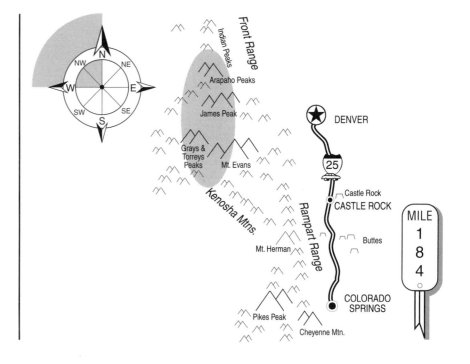

Far to the north are the Indian Peaks, 90 miles (145 km) away. The Continental Divide runs along the tops of these mountains. Many of the peaks are named for Native American tribes.

**Mount Neva** – 12,814 ft (3,906 m). Named by Ellsworth Bethel and James Grafton Rogers for an Arapaho Indian named Neva, a companion of Chief Niwot.

**Santanta Peak** – 11,979 ft (3,651 m). This mountain commemorates the mighty Kiowa warrior Santanta (1830?-1878), which means "White Bear." A stalwart opponent of the white man, Santanta fought hard to defend the Kiowa's land. Three years after his capture, Santanta jumped to his death in a Texas prison.

**South Arapaho Peak** – 13,397 ft (4,083 m). Arapaho means "our people." The tribe is part of the Algonquin family of Native Americans.

**North Arapaho Peak** – 13,502 ft (4,115 m). The Arapaho Peaks were previously known as Mount Edmunds for Commissioner Edmunds of the General Land Office in Washington, D.C.

**Mount Albion** – 12,609 ft (3,843 m). A Celtic word meaning "snowy white" or "alp." This mountain takes its name from an early gold and silver mining settlement nearby. This in turn was named by Scottish miners for their homeland. The peak has also been known as Sheep Mountain.

**Arikaree Peak** – 13,150 ft (4,008 m). Named for the Arikaree (or Arickaree) Indians. *Arikaree* means "horn." The men of the tribe wore headdresses in which they elaborately wrapped their hair in pieces of bone. An older spelling for this mountain is Arikara Peak.

**Kiowa Peak** – 13,276 ft (4,047 m). Named for a fierce Native American indian tribe. *Kiowa* means "principal people." This peak and Mount Albion have been confused in the past.

**Shoshoni Peak** – 12,967 ft (3,952 m). Named for the Shoshoni Native Americans. These nomadic people lived in small groups. Sacagawea, the Indian guide for Lewis and Clark, was a Shoshoni.

**Pawnee Peak** – 12,943 ft (3,945 m).

**Mount Toll** – 12,979 ft (3,956 m). Named for Roger W. Toll (1883-1936), third superintendent of Rocky Mountain National Park. An active member of the Colorado Mountain Club and avid Colorado mountain climber, Toll promoted the building of Trail Ridge Road and the expansion and preservation of the park by including the Indian Peaks area.

**Paiute Peak** – 13,088 ft (3,989 m). Paiute means either "true Ute" or "Water Ute" and is the name for several tribes of Native Americans that reside in Nevada and Utah and are linguistically related to the Colorado Utes. This mountain has also been known as Ute Peak.

**Mount Flora** – 13,132 ft (4,003 m). Historical documents suggest two explanations this peak's name. One account says Dr. Charles Parry, a botanist, named it *flora*—Latin for flower—in 1860, after collecting flowers on the mountain.

Looking northwest, this close-up shows the James Peak group. These mountains are 40 miles (64 km) away. The Continental Divide runs directly across the summit of Mount Flora and onward to James Peak, then northward toward the Wyoming border.

The other story says it is named for Flora Sumner Thomas (1866-1943), the sister-in-law of William Newton Byers, who founded the *Rocky Mountain News*.

**Witter Peak** – 12,884 ft (3,927 m). Named for an obscure individual by the name of Jacob Witter.

**Mount Eva** – 13,130 ft (4,002 m). Named for Eva Ferguson.

**Parry Peak** – 13,391 ft (4,082 m). Named for Dr. Charles C. Parry (1823-1890), a great botanist. Parry named James Peak, Englemann Peak, Grays Peak, and Torreys Peak for other botanists and naturalists that studied Colorado flora and fauna. Breckinridge Peak, farther south, was the original Parry Peak.

**Mount Bancroft** – 13,250 ft (4,039 m). Named for Dr. F. J. Bancroft, an early pioneer and settler of Denver. This mountain has also been known as Lomand's Mountain, Millar's Mountain, and Parry Peak.

**James Peak** – 13,294 ft (4,052 m). Named for Edwin James (1797-1861), the prominent botanist and journalist on the Stephen H. Long expedition of 1820. James is credited with the first recorded ascent of a Colorado peak above 14,000 feet — Pikes Peak. James Peak was named by his admirer, Dr. Charles C. Parry.

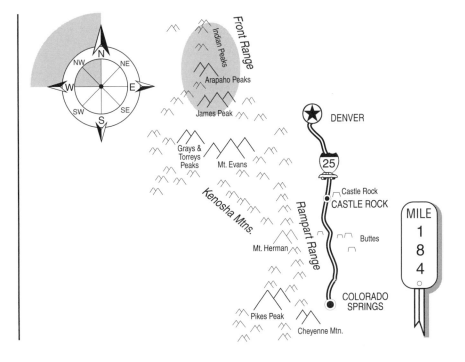

# Northern I-25: Denver to Wyoming

## TRIP HIGHLIGHTS

- Panoramic views of the Continental Divide that greeted early settlers on their travels westward.

- Views of the Front Range, Mummy Range, and Medicine Bow Mountains.

- Longs Peak, the highest point in Rocky Mountain National Park.

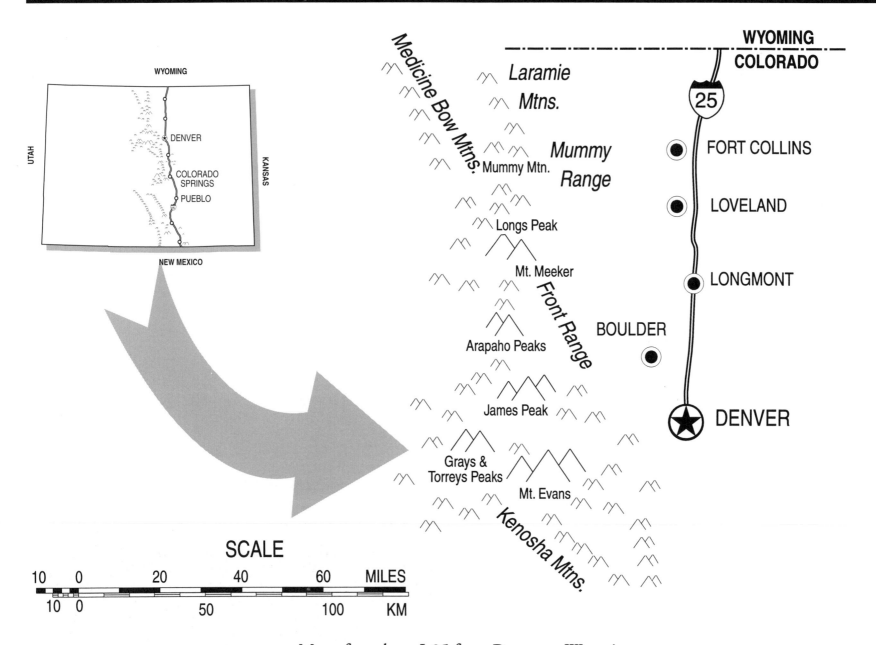

Map of northern I-25 from Denver to Wyoming

This close-up view, taken from mile marker 220, shows the southern end of the Indian Peaks Group. The Arapaho Peaks are prominent mountains from the Denver-area skyline. Many of these mountains are within the Indian Peaks Wilderness area. The Arapaho Peaks are 38 miles (61 km) west-northwest.

**Unnamed** – 12,587 ft (3,837 m).

**Mount Neva** – 12,814 ft (3,906 m). Named in honor of an Arapaho Indian.

**South Arapaho Peak** – 13,397 ft (4,083 m). *Arapaho* means "our people." This Indian tribe is part of the Algonquin family of Native Americans.

**North Arapaho Peak** – 13,502 ft (4,115 m).

**Arikaree Peak** – 13,150 ft (4,008 m).

**Navajo Peak** – 13,409 ft (4,087 m). Named for the Navajo Indians. *Navajo* means "very great farmers."

**Shoshoni Peak** – 12,967 ft (3,952 m).

**Pawnee Peak** – 12,943 ft (3,945 m). Named to honor the Pawnee Indians who lived in eastern Colorado. The word *Pawnee* translates to "horn." Pawnees stiffened their hair with paint and fat, making it stand up like a horn, and dared their enemies to lift their scalps.

**Mount Toll** – 12,979 ft (3,956 m).

**Mount Audubon** – 13,223 ft (4,030 m).

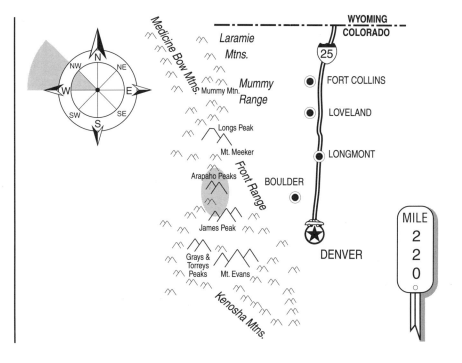

Rampart Range

Rampart Range

Kenosha Mountains

Mount Evans Group

Edwards
Grays & Torreys

This two-page panorama looks west from the Denver suburb of Thornton, at mile marker 220. If the Denver smog is not too bad, you may be able to see Pikes Peak (not in this picture) far to the south, 68 miles (105 km) away. Mount Evans is 39 miles (63 km) southeast. Grays and Torreys Peaks are 47 miles (76 km) away.

**Rampart Range** – The highest point in the Rampart Range is Devils Head 9,748 ft (2,971 m).

**Kenosha Mountains** – The Kenosha Mountains are about 14 miles (23 km) long. This small range trends southeast to northwest. From here, the foothills block the view of the range.

**Mount Evans** – 14,264 ft (4,348 m). Albert Bierstadt, the great western painter, named this mountain Mount Rosalie in honor of his wife. The name was changed to honor the second territorial governor of Colorado, John Evans (1814-1897), on his 81st birthday. Evans also founded the Colorado Seminary of the Methodist Episcopal Church in 1864; it soon closed, but reopened in 1880 as the University of Denver.

**Mount Edwards** – 13,850 ft (4,221 m). Named for Melvin Edwards, the Colorado secretary of state in 1883.

**Torreys Peak** – 14,267 ft (4,349 m). Torreys Peak and its near neighbor Grays Peak were known as "The Ant Hills" by Native Americans. Charles Parry, distinguished botanist, named these mountains after his friends and colleagues Asa Gray (1810-1888) and John Torrey (1796-1873), renowned American botanists.

**Grays Peak** – 14,270 ft (4,349 m). Grays Peak is the 9th-highest peak in Colorado and the highest point on the Continental Divide in the United States or in Canada. Grays and Torreys Peaks are two of the easier 14,000-foot peaks to climb.

**Mount Flora** – 13,132 ft (4,003 m). This peak was also known as Platte Summit.

**Mount Bancroft** – 13,250 ft (4,039 m). Named for Dr. F. J. Bancroft, an early pioneer and settler of Denver. This mountain has also been known as Lomand's Mountain, Millar's Mountain, and Parry Peak.

**James Peak** – 13,294 ft (4,052 m). This peak was named by Dr. Charles C. Parry for Dr. Edwin James, a naturalist and writer.

**Denver** – When William Larimer laid out the streets of Denver in 1858, he aligned them in a northwest to southeast direction, so Longs Peak would fill the vista from 17th Street, the principal business street. Denver-area residents have been frustrated with the traffic flow caused by this decision ever since.

James Peak is 38 miles (61 km) due west. The Indian Peaks Group is about 38 miles away. The distance to Longs Peak is 43 miles (69 km). Farther north, on the horizon, is the Mummy Range, 45 miles (75 km) distant.

**Indian Peaks Group** – The southern end of the Indian Peaks Group is marked by North and South Arapaho Peaks. These two peaks cradle the Arapaho Glacier, the largest snowfield in Colorado. It furnishes about 10 percent of the Boulder city water supply.

**Mount Meeker** – 13,911 ft (4,048 m).

**Longs Peak** – 14,255 ft (4,345 m). The summit of this mountain is larger than a football field, at more than four acres. Historical documents indicate that Arapaho Indians were the first to summit this magnificent peak.

The first white man to climb the peak was Major John Wesley Powell (1834-1902), a one-armed western explorer and geologist. Other members in the first-ascent party included W.H. Powell, L.W. Keplinger, Samual Garman, Ned E. Farrell, John C. Sumner, and William Newton Byers (1831-1903), founder of the *Rocky Mountain News*.

**Mummy Range** – The Arapaho Indians called this range the *nah ou–bāāthā* , meaning "white owls" for the bright, snowy coverings of the mountain sides, especially on Mount Chiquita, Ypsilon Mountain, and Fairchild Mountain.

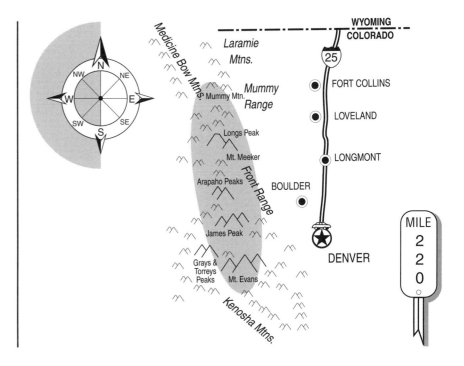

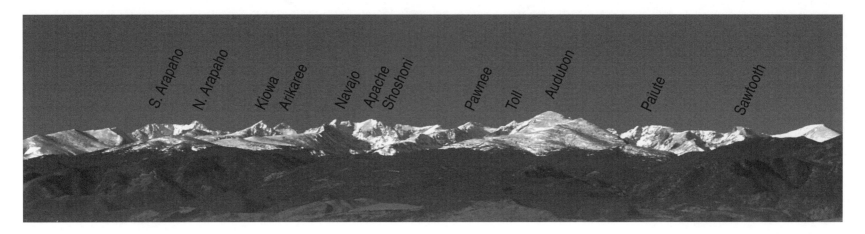

A close-up view of the Indian Peaks looking west-southwest from mile marker 248, just north of Longmont. The mountains in this picture are located along the Continental Divide and are about 35 miles (56 km) away.

**South Arapaho Peak** – 13,397 ft (4,083 m). Ironically, the Arapaho Indians called these peaks "Pawnee Forts" because the Pawnee once defended themselves there.

**North Arapaho Peak** – 13,502 ft (4,115 m).

**Kiowa Peak** – 13,276 ft (4,047 m).

**Arikaree Peak** – 13,150 ft (4,008 m).

**Navajo Peak** – 13,409 ft (4,087 m).

**Apache Peak** – 13,441 ft (4,098 m).

**Shoshoni Peak** – 12,967 ft (3,952 m). This peak, Apache Peak, and nearby George Peak often have had their names transposed.

**Pawnee Peak** – 12,943 ft (3,945 m).

**Mount Toll** – 12,979 ft (3,956 m).

**Mount Audubon** – 13,223 ft (4,030 m). Named for the famous naturalist John James Audubon (1780-1851), for whom the Audubon Society is also named.

**Paiute Peak** – 13,088 ft (3,989 m).

**Sawtooth Mountain** – 12,304 ft (3,750 m). Looking like a tooth on a giant saw blade, this peak is the easternmost point on the entire Continental Divide.

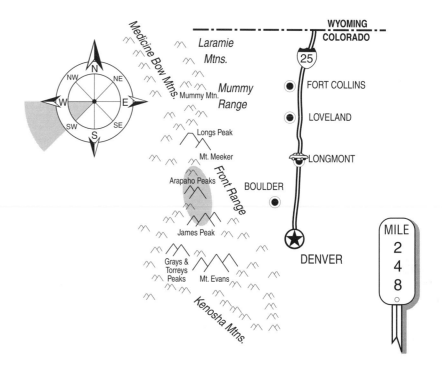

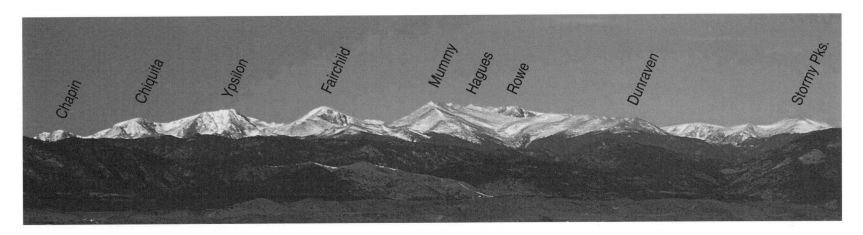

This close-up view looks west from mile marker 248 to some of the beautiful mountains in Rocky Mountain National Park. The Continental Divide runs along the summits and saddles of these peaks. Mummy Mountain is 38 miles (61 km) west.

**Mount Chapin** – 12,454 ft (3,796 m). Named for the mountaineer Frederick H. Chapin (1852-1900), who came to Estes Park and spent two years climbing and exploring the surrounding peaks. He penned *Mountaineering in Colorado*, published in 1889.

**Mount Chiquita** – 13,069 ft (3,983 m).

**Ypsilon Mountain** – 13,514 ft (4,119 m). Named by the wife of Frederick Chapin for spring snowfields high on the eastern face that form the letter "Y." *Ypsilon* is the Greek word for the letter Y.

**Fairchild Mountain** – 13,502 ft (4,115 m). Named for Lucius Fairchild (1831-1896), three-term governor of Wisconsin and minister to Spain. Fairchild visited Denver in 1886. His trip was remembered by his admirers in the name of this mountain.

**Mummy Mountain** – 13,425 ft (4,092 m). Named by W. L. Hallett in 1881. Hallett was an early explorer and mountaineer in the Estes Park region. Hallett thought the mountain looked like an Egyptian sarcophagus when viewed from the south.

**Hagues Peak** – 13,560 ft (4,133 m).

**Rowe Mountain** – 13,184 ft (4,018 m). Named for Israel Rowe, an early settler and explorer of the Estes Park region. Due to a mix-up by the U.S. Board on Geographic Names, two mountains and a glacier in this area are named after Israel Rowe.

**Mount Dunraven** – 12,571 ft (3,832 m).

**Stormy Peaks** – 12,148 ft (3,703 m). Named by a Rocky Mountain National Park ranger for the frequent storms that occur in this area.

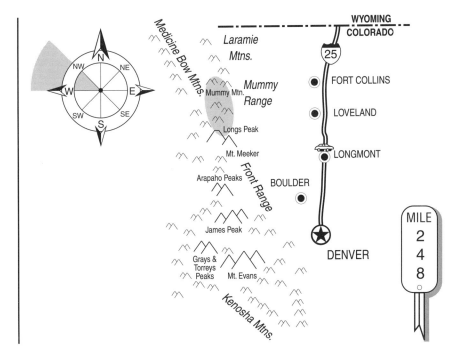

Chapter 5 • Northern I-25: Denver to Wyoming

These two pages show a spectacular panoramic view looking west from mile marker 248. The Continental Divide runs across these mountains, jagging to the west behind Mount Meeker and Longs Peak, before returning to our view at Otis Peak. All of the mountains in this photograph are part of the Front Range. The peaks are about 38 miles away.

**South Arapaho Peak** – 13,397 ft (4,083 m).

**Mount Albion** – 12,609 ft (3,843 m). A Celtic word meaning "snowy white" or "alp." This mountain takes its name from an early gold and silver mining settlement located nearby. This in turn was named by Scottish miners for their homeland. It was once known as Sheep Mountain.

**North Arapaho Peak** – 13,502 ft (4,115 m).

**Kiowa Peak** – 13,276 ft (4,047 m).

**Arikaree Peak** – 13,150 ft (4,008 m).

**Navajo Peak** – 13,409 ft (4,087 m).

**Shoshoni Peak** – 12,967 ft (3,952 m).

**Pawnee Peak** – 12,943 ft (3,945 m).

**Mount Toll** – 12,979 ft (3,956 m).

**Mount Audubon** – 13,223 ft (4,030 m).

**Paiute Peak** – 13,088 ft (3,989 m).

**Sawtooth Mountain** – 12,304 ft (3,750 m).

**St. Vrain Mountain** – 12,162 ft (3,707 m). Named after St. Vrain Creek, which in turn is named for Ceran St. Vrain (1802-1870). The sons of a noble French family, Ceran

and his brother Marcellin were prominent figures in early Colorado history, amassing large land holdings in the southern portion of the state.

**Elk Tooth** – 12,848 ft (3,916 m). Located on the eastern ridge of Ogalalla Peak.

**Ogalalla Peak** – 13,138 ft (4,004 m). Named for a tribe of the Sioux Indians. This peak was formerly known as Ogalalla Horn. It is located behind Copeland Mountain and cannot be seen in the picture above.

**Copeland Mountain** – 13,176 ft (4,016 m). Named for an early settler of Allenspark, a small community southeast of Estes Park. Another name for this mountain was Clarence King Mountain, for Clarence King (1842-1891), the first director of the U.S. Geological Survey.

**Ouzel Peak** – 12,716 ft (3,876 m). Ouzel Peak is named after Ouzel Lake and was once known as Ouzel Lake Peak. Both of these features are named for the water ouzel, a bird commonly known as the water dipper, which dives into rushing streams in search of insects.

**Mahana Peak** – 12,632 ft (3,850 m). *Mahana* is the Taos Indian word for Comanche.

**Isolation Peak** – 13,118 ft (3,998 m). Named for its secluded position on top of the Continental Divide.

**Tanima Peak** – 12,420 ft (3,786 m). The now extinct Tanima tribe of Comanche Indians is remembered in the name of this mountain. *Tanima* means "liver-eater." This peak previously was known as Mount Kirkwood.

Rocky Mountain National Park is about 38 miles west as the crow flies. The park contains 113 named peaks above 10,000 feet (3,048 m) in elevation, and 59 peaks above 12,000 feet (3,658 m).

**Mount Meeker** – 13,911 ft (4,240 m). Named for Nathan Meeker (1814-1879), an agriculturist and Indian agent who had a plan to transform the Northern Ute Indians into farmers. The plan failed miserably. He was killed in the Meeker Massacre in 1879.

**Longs Peak** – 14,255 ft (4,345 m).

**Mount Lady Washington** – 13,281 ft (4,048 m).

**Twin Sisters Mountain** – 11,428 ft (3,483 m).

**Otis Peak** – 12,486 ft (3,806 m).

**Hallett Peak** – 12,713 ft (3,875 m).

**Flattop Mountain** – 12,324 ft (3,756 m). Named for its obvious flat top. This peak stands on the Continental Divide and was formerly known as Table Top Mountain.

**Ptarmigan Point** – 12,363 ft (3,768 m). Named for its close proximity to Ptarmigan Pass.

**Stones Peak** – 12,922 ft (3,939 m).

**Mount Chapin** – 12,454 ft (3,796 m).

**Mount Chiquita** – 13,069 ft (3,983 m).

**Ypsilon Mountain** – 13,514 ft (4,119 m).

**Fairchild Mountain** – 13,502 ft (4,115 m).

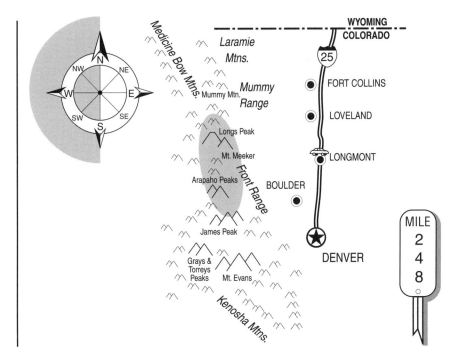

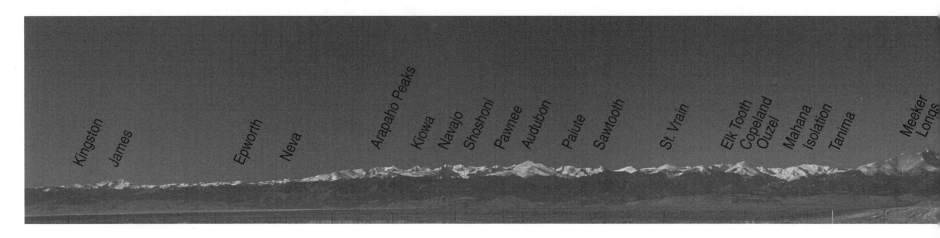

The Colorado Front Range is so-named because travelers from the east were greeted with views of these spectacular peaks, majestically rising above the Great Plains, as their first view of the Rocky Mountains. Today, we can easily travel the length of the Front Range in less than a day—a trip that could take early settlers a week to complete!

**Kingston Peak** – 12,147 ft (3,702 m).

**James Peak** – 13,294 ft (4,052 m).

**Mount Epworth** – 11,843 ft (3,610 m).

**Mount Neva** – 12,814 ft (3,906 m).

**South Arapaho Peak** – 13,397 ft (4,083 m).

**North Arapaho Peak** – 13,502 ft (4,115 m).

**Kiowa Peak** – 13,276 ft (4,047 m).

**Navajo Peak** – 13,409 ft (4,087 m).

**Shoshoni Peak** – 12,967 ft (3,952 m).

**Pawnee Peak** – 12,943 ft (3,945 m).

**Mount Audubon** – 13,223 ft (4,030 m).

**Paiute Peak** – 13,088 ft (3,989 m).

**Sawtooth Mountain** – 12,304 ft (3,750 m).

**St. Vrain Mountain** – 12,162 ft (3,707 m).

**Elk Tooth** – 12,848 ft (3,916 m).

**Copeland Mountain** – 13,176 ft (4,016 m).

**Ouzel Peak** – 12,716 ft (3,876 m).

**Mahana Peak** – 12,632 ft (3,850 m).

**Isolation Peak** – 13,118 ft (3,998 m).

**Tanima Peak** – 12,420 ft (3,786 m).

**Mount Meeker** – 13,911 ft (4,240 m).

**Longs Peak** – 14,255 ft (4,345 m).

**Storm Peak** – 13,326 ft (4,062 m).

**Otis Peak** – 12,486 ft (3,806 m).

The Mummy Range runs from Mount Chapin northward for 20 miles. The peaks in this picture are approximately 35 miles (56 km) away.

**Hallett Peak** – 12,713 ft (3,875 m). The Arapaho name was "Thunder Peak."

**Flattop Mountain** – 12,324 ft (3,756 m). The Arapaho name was "The Big Trail."

**Stones Peak** – 12,922 ft (3,939 m).

**Mount Chapin** – 12,454 ft (3,796 m).

**Mount Chiquita** – 13,069 ft (3,983 m).

**Ypsilon Mountain** – 13,514 ft (4,119 m).

**Fairchild Mountain** – 13,502 ft (4,115 m).

**Mummy Mountain** – 13,425 ft (4,092 m).

**Hagues Peak** – 13,560 ft (4,133 m).

**Rowe Mountain** – 13,184 ft (4,018 m).

**Mount Dunraven** – 12,571 ft (3,832 m).

**Stormy Peaks** – 12,148 ft (3,703 m).

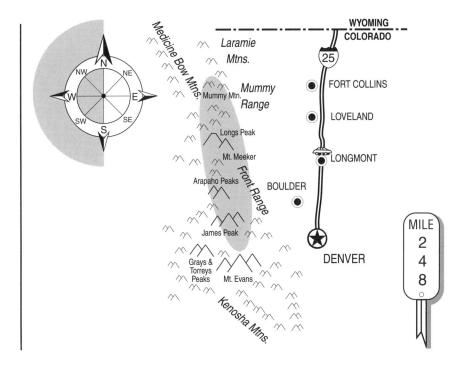

This page and the next show a wide-angle view of the Front Range and Mummy Range from mile marker 248. Mount Evans is 54 miles (87 km) away.

**Mount Evans** – 14,264 ft (4,348 m).

**Thorodin Mountain** – 10,540 ft (3,213 m). Possibly named for the ancient Scandinavian gods of thunder and war, Thor and Odin.

**Grays Peak** – 14,270 ft (4,349 m).

**Torreys Peak** – 14,267 ft (4,349 m). Asa Gray and John Torrey authored the book *Flora of North America*. They named many species of flowers found in the state. Torreys Peak is the 11th-highest point in Colorado.

**Parry Peak** – 13,391 ft (4,082 m). Charles Christopher Parry cataloged many new plants and flowers on his explorations in the Rocky Mountain region. Several flowers are named for the eminent naturalist.

**James Peak** – 13,294 ft (4,052 m). The Arapaho Indians called this peak "The Wolf's Tusks." The meaning is unclear since wolves do not have tusks.

**Indian Peaks Group** – Ellsworth Bethel (1863-1925), a Denver high school teacher, is credited with the idea of naming Front Range peaks after the many tribes of Native Americans associated with Colorado history. While Bethel did not succeed with all of his names, he did secure approval from the U.S. Board on Geographic Names for seven

tribe names on seven Front Range peaks.

**Longs Peak** – 14,255 ft (4,345 m). Longs Peak, the highest point in Rocky Mountain National Park, is named after Major Stephen H. Long (1784-1864). Long was the leader of an early western mapping expedition and was the first to spot the peak in 1820. John Wesley Powell led the first American party to climb the rugged mountain, in August 1868. No doubt, American Indians had scaled it before that time.

The summit of Longs is quite large at more than four acres, and each summer thousands of people attempt to reach its lofty heights. The route is only clear of snow for about eight weeks a year. Snow and ice can make the climb extremely dangerous. The climb generally takes two days, and requires basic mountaineering skills and good physical condition.

Longs sister mountain, Mount Meeker, is just to the left of Longs Peak and rises to 13,911 feet.

**Twin Sisters Mountain** – 11,428 ft (3,483 m). From the east, this mountain appears to have twin summits. It was previously known as Lily Mountain.

**Otis Peak** – 12,486 ft (3,806 m). Otis Peak was named by Frederick Chapin for

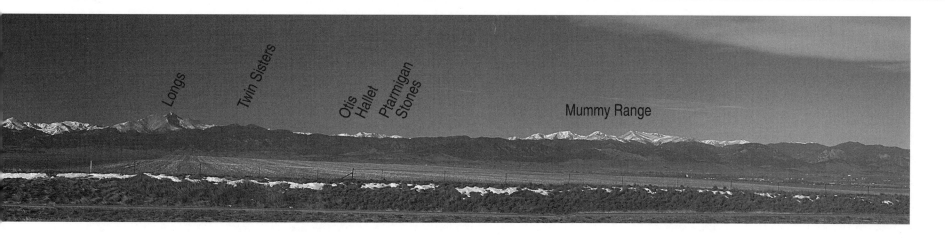

This panorama view to the west encompasses more than 120 miles (193 km). Longs Peak is 34 miles (55 km) due west. Most of the Mummy Range can be seen farther north.

Dr. Edward Osgood Otis (1848-?), a climbing companion of Chapin's.

**Hallett Peak** – 12,713 ft (3,875 m). This distinctive and photogenic mountain was named by Frederick Chapin for his friend and climbing partner William L. Hallett (1851-1941). Hallett was one of the 18 founding members of Colorado's first climbing organization, the Rocky Mountain Club. Hallett was an engineer and cattle rancher.

**Ptarmigan Point** – 12,363 ft (3,768 m). The ptarmigan is one of the few birds that can live above timberline year-round. It's a ground nester with feathers that grow down to its toes, so they act like snowshoes. The bird is extremely well camouflaged.

**Stones Peak** – 12,922 ft (3,939 m). Named for Professor G. M. Stone (1841-1917), who climbed with Frederick Chapin and studied the geology of the Estes Park region. Stones Peak and nearby Mount Julian were known by the Arapaho Native Americans as the "Bear Paws" because of the many bears that inhabited this area.

**Mummy Range** – Hagues Peak, 13,560 ft (4,133 m) is the high point of the Mummy Range.

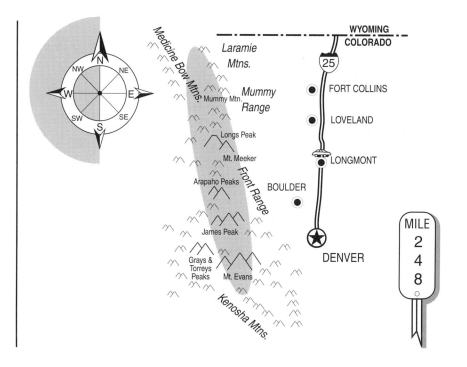

This close-up view from mile marker 259 shows Mummy Mountain and its neighbors in the Mummy Range. These isolated peaks were called the "*White Owls*" by Native Americans. The peaks are about 34 miles (55 km) west.

**Mount Chiquita** – 13,069 ft (3,983 m). This mountain may be named after an early-1900s book titled *Chiquita an American Novel: The Romance of a Ute Chief's Daughter.*

**Ypsilon Mountain** – 13,514 ft (4,119 m).

**Fairchild Mountain** – 13,502 ft (4,115 m).

**Mummy Mountain** – 13,425 ft (4,092 m).

**Hagues Peak** – 13,560 ft (4,133 m). Named for Arnold Hague (1840-1917) and his brother James. Both men worked with Clarence King (see Copeland Mountain) on the survey of the 40th parallel.

**Rowe Mountain** – 13,184 ft (4,018 m).

**Mount Dunraven** – 12,571 ft (3,832 m). Named for the Irish Earl of Dunraven (1841-1926), who fell in love with Estes Park and what would become Rocky Mountain National Park. The earl, a wealthy British nobleman, fiendishly attempted to turn the park and surrounding countryside into his private hunting preserve. At one time the earl owned close to 15,000 acres. Later, the earl lost rights to most of the land and sold the rest of his holdings.

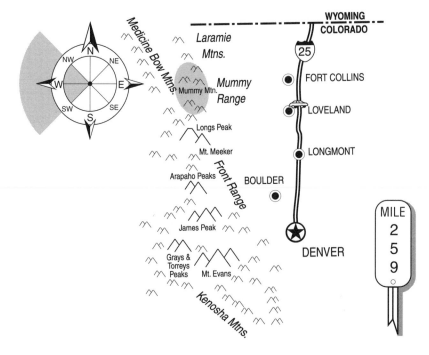

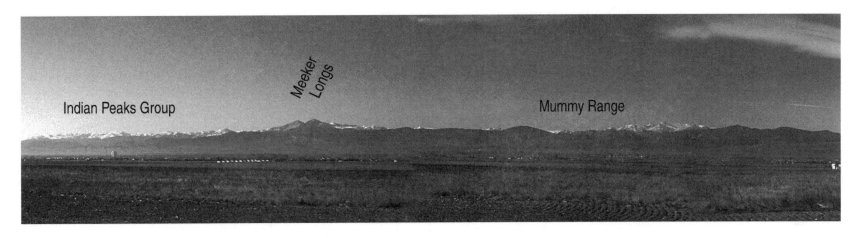

Indian Peaks Group

Meeker
Longs

Mummy Range

From mile marker 259, this view looks from the southwest to the west. The Indian Peaks are about 44 miles (71 km) southwest. Mount Meeker and Longs Peak are 35 miles (56 km) southwest, and the Mummy Range is 34 miles (55 km) west.

**Indian Peaks Group** – 13,502 ft (4,115 m).

**Mount Meeker** – 13,911 ft (4,240 m).

**Longs Peak** – 14,255 ft (4,345 m). The east face of this mountain is called the Diamond face for its sheer diamond-shaped wall nearly 1,000 feet (304 m) high. Technical climbers from around the world come to climb this imposing and beautiful face, visible from the highway.

**Mummy Range** – The Mummy Range is probably named for Mummy Mountain, one of the predominant mountains in this short range. The Mummy Range runs from Mount Chapin north to Crown Point, and is about 20 miles (32 km) long.

**Mummy Range** – The 20 named summits of the Mummy Range include Mount Chapin, Mount Chiquita, Ypsilon Mountain, Mount Tileston, Bighorn Mountain, Fairchild Mountain, Flatiron Mountain, Desolation Peaks, Mummy Mountain, Mount Dunraven, Hagues Peak, Rowe Peak, Rowe Mountain, Skull Point, Sugarloaf Mountain, Stormy Peaks, Ramsey Peak, Fall Mountain, Comanche Peak, and Crown Point.

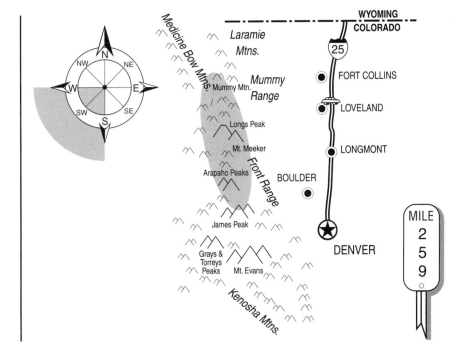

From mile marker 281 at the Owl Canyon Road exit north of Fort Collins, this beautiful panorama looks to the southwest. The mountain on this side of Longs Peak and Mount Meeker is Mount Lady Washington. Longs Peak is about 45 miles (72 km) southwest.

**Indian Peaks Group** – 13,502 ft (4,115 m).

**Mount Meeker** – 13,911 ft (4,240 m).

**Longs Peak** – 14,255 ft (4,345 m). Historical documents indicate Arapaho Indians climbed the peak in 1859, nine years before the first white man was to climb it.

A great Arapaho medicine man by the name of "Old Man Gun" reportedly trapped bald eagles on the summit of this mountain. Gun would scale the mountain at night so the eagles would not see him. It was said that a pair of moccasins would wear out in only three hours while he climbed the rough mountain slopes. Hiding in a shallow hole, he would place a stuffed coyote smeared with animal fat above the trap and wait patiently for an eagle. With their keen eyesight, eagles could see the bait from many miles away. When the eagle landed, Gun would jump up and grab and bind the eagle's feet.

Eagle feathers were used by the Indians for their headdresses and in ceremonies.

**Mount Lady Washington** – 13,281 ft (4,048 m). Anna Dickinson, an early female climber in the Estes Park region (see Mount Dickinson), most likely named this moun-tain for a favorite peak of hers in New Hampshire, Mount Washington. According to Louisa Arps in *High Country Names*, the "lady" may have been added by Ralph Meeker as a compliment to Miss Dickinson.

**Storm Peak** – 13,326 ft (4,062 m). Enos Mills, the father of Rocky Mountain National Park, renamed this mountain Storm Peak for the frequent thunderstorms that develop. The mountain was previously known as Velies Peak, after Jacob W. Velie (1829-1908), who explored Colorado with the famous botanist Dr. Charles C. Parry.

**McHenrys Peak** – 13,327 ft (4,062 m). Abner Sprague, an early settler and pioneer in the Estes Park region, named this mountain for B. F. McHenry ,who spent three summers in the region in the early 1890s.

**Mount Dickinson** – 11,831 ft (3,606 m). Named for Anna E. Dickinson (1842-1932), the first woman to climb Longs Peak. She summited the mountain in September 1873 with members of the Hayden Survey.

**Signal Mountain** – 11,262 ft (3,433 m). Early settlers reportedly saw smoke signals emanating from this mountain top. The Arapaho Indians knew this mountain as "Wolf Ridge" and as "Squaw Club."

This is the northern end of the Mummy Range. Crown Point is 35 miles (56 km) west. North of the Mummy Range, and farther west, are the Medicine Bow Mountains. The Medicine Bow range runs northward into Wyoming.

**Mount Dunraven** – 12,571 ft (3,832 m). Much of the Estes Park land holdings that the Earl of Dunraven once owned were sold to Freelan Oscar Stanley (1849-1940), who, along with his brother, invented and manufactured the Stanley Steamer. Stanley built a grand hotel in Estes Park. The old hotel inspired novelist Stephen King to write his best-selling book *The Shining*.

**Sugarloaf Mountain** – 12,120 ft (3,694 m).

**Ramsey Peak** – 11,582 ft (3,530 m). Named for Hugh B. Ramsey (1862-?), an early resident of Loveland.

**Fall Mountain** – 12,258 ft (3,736 m). Named for Fall Creek, which runs down this mountain. Fall Creek contains a long drop or "fall."

**Comanche Peak** – 12,702 ft (3,872 m). Although it seems unlikely, one source traces the name of this mountain to a Ute Indian chief by the name of Comanche. Elsewhere, the name is attributed to the plains tribe of Comanche Indians.

**Crown Point** – 11,463 ft (3,494 m). The northernmost mountain in the Mummy Range.

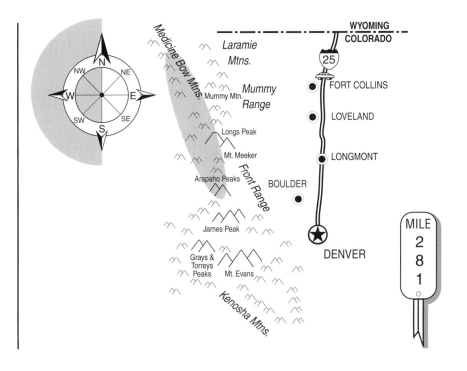

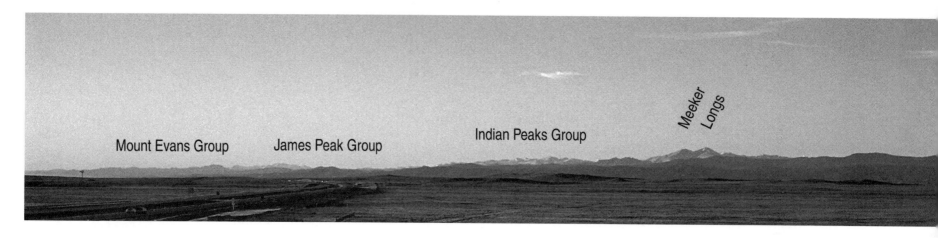

Mount Evans Group    James Peak Group    Indian Peaks Group    Meeker    Longs

This panorama looks south and west from mile marker 293, just six miles from the Colorado-Wyoming border. Far to the south, on the horizon, is the Mount Evans Group of the Front Range, 95 miles (153 km) away. Longs Peak is 56 miles away.

**Mount Evans Group** – 14,264 ft (4,348 m) Mount Evans is the principal peak in this small group of mountains. The Evans group is part of the Colorado Front Range.

**Indian Peaks Group** – 13,502 ft (4,115 m).

**Mount Meeker** – 13,911 ft (4,240 m).

**Longs Peak** – 14,255 ft (4,345 m). Before the white man renamed this peak, it was known to the Arapahos as *Nesótaieux*, meaning "Two Guides." Early French trappers called it *Les Deux Oreilles*— "The Two Ears." The names refer to Longs Peak and its neighbor Mount Meeker. These two looming landmarks were often used for route finding.

**Pikes Peak** – If the lighting conditions are just right, and with keen eyesight, the silhouette of the Pikes Peak Massif can be seen far to the south, more than 140 miles (225 km) away!

**Mount Dickinson** – 11,831 ft (3,606 m). Anna E. Dickinson climbed and wrote about the Colorado mountains. She also traveled and climbed with the Hayden Geographical Survey. Anna and her brother Reverend John Dickinson were with the Hayden expedition when it scaled and charted Longs Peak.

**Mount Dunraven** – 12,571 ft (3,832 m). Named for Windham Thomas Wyndham-Quinn (1841-1926), Fourth Earl of Dunraven. He was a hunter, sportsman, and wealthy nobleman. He acquired much of the Estes Park region through unscrupulous means.

Abner Sprague, an early settler and distinguished resident of Estes Park, speculated that without the Earl of Dunraven's selfish desire to own the land around Estes Park, this valuable land might never have been available later for the formation of Rocky Mountain National Park.

**Sugarloaf Mountain** – 12,120 ft (3,694 m). There are more than 30 named summits in Colorado alone called "sugar loaf." With the popularity of purified sugar, this word has faded into obscurity along with the conical-shaped sugar loaves of yesteryear.

**Ramsey Peak** – 11,582 ft (3,530 m).

**Fall Mountain** – 12,258 ft (3,736 m).

**Comanche Peak** – 12,702 ft (3,872 m). This peak was mapped and named on the U.S. Geological Exploration of the 40th parallel in 1876, led by Clarence King.

The smaller mountains and hills in the foreground are part of the Laramie Mountains. Behind them are the Rawahs and the Medicine Bow Mountains. Clark and the Rawah Peaks are 45 miles (72 km) away.

**Crown Point** – 11,463 ft (3,494 m).

**Clark Peak** – 12,951 ft (3,947 m). Named for William Clark (1770-1838) of the Lewis and Clark expedition. The Native American name for this peak is Elk Horn. Clark Peak is the highest point in the Rawah Range.

**South Rawah Peak** – 12,644 ft (3,854 m). *Rawah* is the Ute Indian word for "wilderness." In 1980 Congress set aside a portion of the pristine land in this area to be preserved by wilderness legislation. The Rawah Wilderness contains more than 73,000 acres.

**North Rawah Peak** – 12,473 ft (3,802 m). The Rawah Range is actually the southernmost section of the Medicine Bow Mountains. It runs from Cameron Pass, just north of the Never Summer Mountains, north-northwest for 15 miles.

 **Medicine Bow Mountains** – Clark Peak and the Rawah Peaks are part of the Medicine Bow Mountains. One old tale says this range got its name because Native Americans made superior bows from the ash trees in this range. These bows were "good medicine."

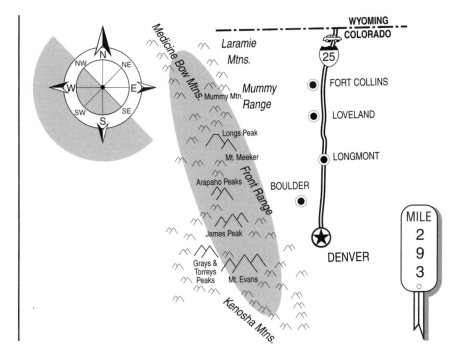

# Alphabetical List of Mountains in this Volume

*(Elevations in feet)*

| Summit | Elevation | Summit | Elevation | Summit | Elevation |
|---|---|---|---|---|---|
| Albion, Mount | 12,609 | Bierstadt, Mount | 14,060 | Clark Peak | 12,951 |
| Almagre Mountain | 12,367 | Black Hills | 7,516 | Cleveland Peak | 13,414 |
| Apache Peak | 13,441 | Black Mountain | 10,132 | Colony Baldy | 13,705 |
| Arapaho Peak, North | 13,502 | Blanca Peak | 14,345 | Comanche Peak | 12,702 |
| Arapaho Peak, South | 13,397 | Blizzardine Peak | 11,910 | Cooper Mountain | 9,146 |
| Arikaree Peak | 13,150 | Blodgett Peak | 9,423 | Copeland Mountain | 13,176 |
| Arthur, Mount | 10,807 | Blueberry Peak | 12,005 | Crestone Needle | 14,197 |
| Audubon, Mount | 13,223 | Broken Hand Peak | 13,573 | Crestone Peak | 14,294 |
| Badito Cone | 8,942 | California Peak | 13,849 | Crown Point | 11,463 |
| Bald Mountain | 11,340 | Cameron Cone | 10,707 | Crown Point | 9,922 |
| Baldy | 8,068 | Carbonate Mountain | 12,308 | Cuatro Peak | 13,487 |
| Bancroft, Mount | 13,250 | Castle Rock | 6,586 | Culebra Peak | 14,047 |
| Bandit Peak | 12,444 | Castle Rocks | 6,480 | Dawson Butte | 7,481 |
| Barela Mesa | 8,720 | Chapin, Mount | 12,454 | De Anza Peak | 13,333 |
| Beaubien Peak | 13,184 | Chautauqua Mountain | 8,352 | Dickinson, Mount | 11,831 |
| Beck Mountain | 10,749 | Cheyenne Mountain | 9,565 | Dunraven, Mount | 12,571 |
| Berg | 9,543 | Chiquita, Mount | 13,069 | Edwards, Mount | 13,850 |

| Summit | Elevation | Summit | Elevation | Summit | Elevation |
|---|---|---|---|---|---|
| Elk Tooth | 12,848 | James Peak | 13,294 | Ormes Peak | 9,727 |
| Ellingwood Point | 14,042 | Kineo Mountain | 9,478 | Otis Peak | 12,486 |
| Epaulet Mountain | 13,523 | Kingston Peak | 12,147 | Ouzel Peak | 12,716 |
| Epworth, Mount | 11,843 | Kiowa Peak | 13,276 | Paiute Peak | 13,088 |
| Eva, Mount | 13,130 | Kit Carson Mountain | 14,165 | Park Mountain | 11,670 |
| Evans, Mount | 14,264 | Kruger Mountain | 9,498 | Parry Peak | 13,391 |
| Fairchild Mountain | 13,502 | Lady Washington, Mount | 13,281 | Pawnee Peak | 12,943 |
| Fall Mountain | 12,258 | Larkspur Butte | 7,535 | Pico Aislado | 13,611 |
| Fishers Peak | 9,627 | Lindsey, Mount | 14,042 | Pikes Peak | 14,110 |
| Fishers Peak Mesa | 9,626 | Little Bear Peak | 14,037 | Point of Rocks | 8,130 |
| Flattop Mountain | 12,324 | Little Sheep Mountain | 9,610 | Prospect Point (approx.) | 6,400 |
| Flora, Mount | 13,132 | Logan, Mount | 12,871 | Ptarmigan Point | 12,363 |
| Francisco Peak | 13,135 | Lomo Liso Mountain | 13,128 | Purgatoire Peak | 13,676 |
| Garfield, Mount | 10,900 | Longs Peak | 14,255 | Ramsey Peak | 11,582 |
| Goliath Peak | 12,216 | Mahana Peak | 12,632 | Raspberry Butte | 7,680 |
| Gray Back Peak | 9,348 | Manitou, Mount | 9,450 | Raspberry Mountain | 8,634 |
| Gray Wolf Mountain | 13,602 | Marble Mountain | 13,266 | Raton Mesa | 9,064 |
| Grays Peak | 14,270 | Mariquita Peak | 13,405 | Rattlesnake Butte | 7,570 |
| Green Mountain | 11,400 | Maxwell, Mount | 13,335 | Rawah Peak, North | 12,473 |
| Greenhorn Mountain | 12,347 | McHenrys Peak | 13,327 | Rawah Peak, South | 12,644 |
| Hagues Peak | 13,560 | Meeker, Mount | 13,911 | Red Mountain | 13,908 |
| Hallett Peak | 12,713 | Mestas, Mount | 11,569 | Rogers Peak | 13,391 |
| Hamilton Peak | 13,658 | Milwaukee Peak | 13,522 | Rosa, Mount | 11,499 |
| Haystack Mountain | 11,495 | Miranda Peak | 13,468 | Rosalie Peak | 13,575 |
| Herard, Mount | 13,350 | Monkey Face | 7,719 | Rough Mountain | 11,138 |
| Herman, Mount | 9,063 | Mummy Mountain | 13,425 | Rowe Mountain | 13,184 |
| Hogback, The | 6,584 | Music Mountain | 13,355 | Rudolph Mountain | 10,334 |
| Horns, The | 9,212 | Napoleon Peak | 11,866 | Rugby Rock | 6,800 |
| Horseshoe Mesa | 8,802 | Navajo Peak | 13,409 | Sachett Mountain | 12,560 |
| Huerfano Butte | 6,166 | Nemrick Butte | 7,465 | St. Charles Peak | 11,784 |
| Humboldt Peak | 14,064 | Neva, Mount | 12,814 | St. Vrain Mountain | 12,162 |
| Iron Mountain | 11,411 | North Peak | 12,220 | Santanta Peak | 11,979 |
| Iron Nipple | 13,360 | North Peak | 9,368 | Sawtooth Mountain | 12,304 |
| Isolation Peak | 13,118 | Ogalalla Peak | 13,138 | Scraggy Peaks | 9,198 |

| Summit | Elevation | Summit | Elevation |
|---|---|---|---|
| Sheep Mountain | 12,397 | Warren, Mount | 13,307 |
| Sheep Mountain | 10,635 | Witter Peak | 12,884 |
| Shoshoni Peak | 12,967 | Ypsilon Mountain | 13,514 |
| Signal Mountain | 11,262 | Zwischen, Mount | 12,006 |
| Silver Mountain | 10,522 | | |
| Simpsons Rest | 6,420 | | |
| Slide Mountain | 12,306 | | |
| Snowslide Mountain | 11,664 | | |
| South Peak | 9,321 | | |
| Spalding, Mount | 13,842 | | |
| Spanish Peak, East | 12,683 | | |
| Spanish Peak, West | 13,626 | | |
| Sperry Mountain | 10,935 | | |
| St. Peters Dome | 9,665 | | |
| State Line Peak | 12,867 | | |
| Stones Peak | 12,922 | | |
| Storm Peak | 13,326 | | |
| Stormy Peaks | 12,148 | | |
| Stove Mountain | 9,782 | | |
| Stull Mountain | 10,000 | | |
| Sugar Loaf | 7,456 | | |
| Sugarloaf Mountain | 12,120 | | |
| Sundance Mountain | 8,255 | | |
| Tanima Peak | 12,420 | | |
| Teddys Peak | 12,402 | | |
| Tenney Crags | 10,094 | | |
| Thorodin Mountain | 10,540 | | |
| Tijeras Peak | 13,604 | | |
| Toll, Mount | 12,979 | | |
| Torreys Peak | 14,267 | | |
| Trinchera Peak | 13,517 | | |
| Twin Sisters Mountain | 11,428 | | |
| Vermejo Peak | 13,723 | | |
| Vigil, Mount | 10,073 | | |

# Mountains in this Volume by Elevation

*(Elevations in feet)*

| Summit | Elevation | Summit | Elevation | Summit | Elevation |
|---|---|---|---|---|---|
| Blanca Peak | 14,345 | Mount Edwards | 13,850 | Ypsilon Mountain | 13,514 |
| Crestone Peak | 14,294 | California Peak | 13,849 | Fairchild Mountain | 13,502 |
| Grays Peak | 14,270 | Mount Spalding | 13,842 | North Arapaho Peak | 13,502 |
| Torreys Peak | 14,267 | Vermejo Peak | 13,723 | Cuatro Peak | 13,487 |
| Mount Evans | 14,264 | Colony Baldy | 13,705 | Miranda Peak | 13,468 |
| Longs Peak | 14,255 | Purgatoire Peak | 13,676 | Apache Peak | 13,441 |
| Crestone Needle | 14,197 | Hamilton Peak | 13,658 | Mummy Mountain | 13,425 |
| Kit Carson Mountain | 14,165 | West Spanish Peak | 13,626 | Cleveland Peak | 13,414 |
| Pikes Peak | 14,110 | Pico Aislado | 13,611 | Navajo Peak | 13,409 |
| Humboldt Peak | 14,064 | Tijeras Peak | 13,604 | Mariquita Peak | 13,405 |
| Mount Bierstadt | 14,060 | Gray Wolf Mountain | 13,602 | South Arapaho Peak | 13,397 |
| Culebra Peak | 14,047 | Rosalie Peak | 13,575 | Parry Peak | 13,391 |
| Ellingwood Point | 14,042 | Broken Hand Peak | 13,573 | Rogers Peak | 13,391 |
| Mount Lindsey | 14,042 | Hagues Peak | 13,560 | Iron Nipple | 13,360 |
| Little Bear Peak | 14,037 | Epaulet Mountain | 13,523 | Music Mountain | 13,355 |
| Mount Meeker | 13,911 | Milwaukee Peak | 13,522 | Mount Herard | 13,350 |
| Red Mountain | 13,908 | Trinchera Peak | 13,517 | Mount Maxwell | 13,335 |

| Summit | Elevation | Summit | Elevation | Summit | Elevation |
|---|---|---|---|---|---|
| De Anza Peak | 13,333 | Comanche Peak | 12,702 | Mount Dickinson | 11,831 |
| McHenrys Peak | 13,327 | East Spanish Peak | 12,683 | St. Charles Peak | 11,784 |
| Storm Peak | 13,326 | South Rawah Peak | 12,644 | Park Mountain | 11,670 |
| Mount Warren | 13,307 | Mahana Peak | 12,632 | Snowslide Mountain | 11,664 |
| James Peak | 13,294 | Mount Albion | 12,609 | Ramsey Peak | 11,582 |
| Mount Lady Washington | 13,281 | Mount Dunraven | 12,571 | Mount Mestas | 11,569 |
| Kiowa Peak | 13,276 | Sachett Mountain | 12,560 | Mount Rosa | 11,499 |
| Marble Mountain | 13,266 | Otis Peak | 12,486 | Haystack Mountain | 11,495 |
| Mount Bancroft | 13,250 | North Rawah Peak | 12,473 | Crown Point | 11,463 |
| Mount Audubon | 13,223 | Mount Chapin | 12,454 | Twin Sisters Mountain | 11,428 |
| Beaubien Peak | 13,184 | Bandit Peak | 12,444 | Iron Mountain | 11,411 |
| Rowe Mountain | 13,184 | Tanima Peak | 12,420 | Green Mountain | 11,400 |
| Copeland Mountain | 13,176 | Teddys Peak | 12,402 | Bald Mountain | 11,340 |
| Arikaree Peak | 13,150 | Sheep Mountain | 12,397 | Signal Mountain | 11,262 |
| Ogalalla Peak | 13,138 | Almagre Mountain | 12,367 | Rough Mountain | 11,138 |
| Francisco Peak | 13,135 | Ptarmigan Point | 12,363 | Sperry Mountain | 10,935 |
| Mount Flora | 13,132 | Greenhorn Mountain | 12,347 | Mount Garfield | 10,900 |
| Mount Eva | 13,130 | Flattop Mountain | 12,324 | Mount Arthur | 10,807 |
| Lomo Liso Mountain | 13,128 | Carbonate Mountain | 12,308 | Beck Mountain | 10,749 |
| Isolation Peak | 13,118 | Slide Mountain | 12,306 | Cameron Cone | 10,707 |
| Paiute Peak | 13,088 | Sawtooth Mountain | 12,304 | Sheep Mountain | 10,635 |
| Mount Chiquita | 13,069 | Fall Mountain | 12,258 | Thorodin Mountain | 10,540 |
| Mount Toll | 12,979 | North Peak | 12,220 | Silver Mountain | 10,522 |
| Shoshoni Peak | 12,967 | Goliath Peak | 12,216 | Rudolph Mountain | 10,334 |
| Clark Peak | 12,951 | St. Vrain Mountain | 12,162 | Black Mountain | 10,132 |
| Pawnee Peak | 12,943 | Stormy Peaks | 12,148 | Tenney Crags | 10,094 |
| Stones Peak | 12,922 | Kingston Peak | 12,147 | Mount Vigil | 10,073 |
| Witter Peak | 12,884 | Sugarloaf Mountain | 12,120 | Stull Mountain | 10,000 |
| Mount Logan | 12,871 | Mount Zwischen | 12,006 | Crown Point | 9,922 |
| State Line Peak | 12,867 | Blueberry Peak | 12,005 | Stove Mountain | 9,782 |
| Elk Tooth | 12,848 | Santanta Peak | 11,979 | Ormes Peak | 9,727 |
| Mount Neva | 12,814 | Blizzardine Peak | 11,910 | St. Peters Dome | 9,665 |
| Ouzel Peak | 12,716 | Napoleon Peak | 11,866 | Fishers Peak | 9,627 |
| Hallett Peak | 12,713 | Mount Epworth | 11,843 | Fishers Peak Mesa | 9,626 |

| Summit | Elevation | Summit | Elevation |
|---|---|---|---|
| Little Sheep Mountain | 9,610 | Castle Rocks | 6,480 |
| Cheyenne Mountain | 9,565 | Simpsons Rest | 6,420 |
| Berg | 9,543 | Prospect Point (approx.) | 6,400 |
| Kruger Mountain | 9,498 | Huerfano Butte | 6,166 |
| Kineo Mountain | 9,478 | | |
| Mount Manitou | 9,450 | | |
| Blodgett Peak | 9,423 | | |
| North Peak | 9,368 | | |
| Gray Back Peak | 9,348 | | |
| South Peak | 9,321 | | |
| The Horns | 9,212 | | |
| Scraggy Peaks | 9,198 | | |
| Cooper Mountain | 9,146 | | |
| Raton Mesa | 9,064 | | |
| Mount Herman | 9,063 | | |
| Badito Cone | 8,942 | | |
| Horseshoe Mesa | 8,802 | | |
| Barela Mesa | 8,720 | | |
| Raspberry Mountain | 8,634 | | |
| Chautauqua Mountain | 8,352 | | |
| Sundance Mountain | 8,255 | | |
| Point of Rocks | 8,130 | | |
| Baldy | 8,068 | | |
| Monkey Face | 7,719 | | |
| Raspberry Butte | 7,680 | | |
| Rattlesnake Butte | 7,570 | | |
| Larkspur Butte | 7,535 | | |
| Black Hills | 7,516 | | |
| Dawson Butte | 7,481 | | |
| Nemrick Butte | 7,465 | | |
| Sugar Loaf | 7,456 | | |
| Rugby Rock | 6,800 | | |
| Castle Rock | 6,586 | | |
| The Hogback | 6,584 | | |

# 500 Highest Named Summits in Colorado

*(Elevations in feet)*

| | Summit | Elevation | | Summit | Elevation | | Summit | Elevation |
|---|---|---|---|---|---|---|---|---|
| 1. | Mount Elbert | 14,433 | 25. | El Diente Peak | 14,159 | 49. | Redcloud Peak | 14,034 |
| 2. | Mount Massive | 14,421 | 26. | Maroon Peak | 14,156 | 50. | Conundrum Peak | 14,022 |
| 3. | Mount Harvard | 14,420 | 27. | Tabeguache Peak | 14,155 | 51. | Pyramid Peak | 14,018 |
| 4. | La Plata Peak | 14,361 | 28. | Mount Oxford | 14,153 | 52. | Wilson Peak | 14,017 |
| 5. | Blanca Peak | 14,345 | 29. | Mount Sneffels | 14,150 | 53. | Wetterhorn Peak | 14,015 |
| 6. | Uncompahgre Peak | 14,309 | 30. | Mount Democrat | 14,148 | 54. | North Maroon Peak | 14,014 |
| 7. | Crestone Peak | 14,294 | 31. | Capitol Peak | 14,130 | 55. | San Luis Peak | 14,014 |
| 8. | Mount Lincoln | 14,286 | 32. | Pikes Peak | 14,110 | 56. | Huron Peak | 14,005 |
| 9. | Grays Peak | 14,270 | 33. | Snowmass Mountain | 14,092 | 57. | Mount of the Holy Cross | 14,005 |
| 10. | Mount Antero | 14,269 | 34. | Mount Eolus | 14,083 | 58. | Sunshine Peak | 14,001 |
| 11. | Torreys Peak | 14,267 | 35. | Windom Peak | 14,082 | 59. | Grizzly Peak | 13,988 |
| 12. | Castle Peak | 14,265 | 36. | Challenger Point | 14,080 | 60. | Stewart Peak | 13,983 |
| 13. | Quandary Peak | 14,265 | 37. | Mount Columbia | 14,073 | 61. | Pigeon Peak | 13,972 |
| 14. | Mount Evans | 14,264 | 38. | Missouri Mountain | 14,067 | 62. | Mount Ouray | 13,971 |
| 15. | Longs Peak | 14,255 | 39. | Humboldt Peak | 14,064 | 63. | Fletcher Mountain | 13,951 |
| 16. | Mount Wilson | 14,246 | 40. | Mount Bierstadt | 14,060 | 64. | Gemini Peak | 13,951 |
| 17. | Mount Cameron | 14,238 | 41. | Sunlight Peak | 14,059 | 65. | Pacific Peak | 13,950 |
| 18. | Mount Shavano | 14,229 | 42. | Handies Peak | 14,048 | 66. | Cathedral Peak | 13,943 |
| 19. | Mount Belford | 14,197 | 43. | Culebra Peak | 14,047 | 67. | Mount Hope | 13,933 |
| 20. | Crestone Needle | 14,197 | 44. | Ellingwood Point | 14,042 | 68. | Mount Adams | 13,931 |
| 21. | Mount Princeton | 14,197 | 45. | Mount Lindsey | 14,042 | 69. | Gladstone Peak | 13,913 |
| 22. | Mount Yale | 14,196 | 46. | North Eolus | 14,039 | 70. | Mount Meeker | 13,911 |
| 23. | Mount Bross | 14,172 | 47. | Little Bear Peak | 14,037 | 71. | Casco Peak | 13,908 |
| 24. | Kit Carson Mountain | 14,165 | 48. | Mount Sherman | 14,036 | 72. | Red Mountain | 13,908 |

| Summit | Elevation | Summit | Elevation | Summit | Elevation |
|---|---|---|---|---|---|
| 73. Emerald Peak | 13,904 | 121. Vermejo Peak | 13,723 | 169. Twin Peaks | 13,580 |
| 74. Horseshoe Mountain | 13,898 | 122. Pole Creek Mountain | 13,716 | 170. Chiefs Head Peak | 13,579 |
| 75. Vermilion Peak | 13,894 | 123. Silver Mountain | 13,714 | 171. Mount Evans | 13,577 |
| 76. Mount Buckskin | 13,865 | 124. Twining Peak | 13,711 | 172. Gravel Mountain | 13,577 |
| 77. The Three Apostles | 13,863 | 125. Colony Baldy | 13,705 | 173. Greylock Mountain | 13,575 |
| 78. Jones Mountain | 13,860 | 126. Needle Mountains Peak Six | 13,705 | 174. Rosalie Peak | 13,575 |
| 79. Clinton Peak | 13,857 | 127. Needle Mountains Peak Thirteen | 13,705 | 175. Mount Parnassus | 13,574 |
| 80. Dyer Mountain | 13,855 | 128. Glacier Point | 13,704 | 176. Broken Hand Peak | 13,573 |
| 81. Crystal Peak | 13,852 | 129. Treasurevault Mountain | 13,701 | 177. Weston Peak | 13,572 |
| 82. Traver Peak | 13,852 | 130. Baldy Alto | 13,698 | 178. Jones Peak | 13,571 |
| 83. Mount Edwards | 13,850 | 131. Monitor Peak | 13,695 | 179. Carbonate Mountain | 13,570 |
| 84. California Peak | 13,849 | 132. Gilpin Peak | 13,694 | 180. Crown Mountain | 13,569 |
| 85. Mount Oklahoma | 13,845 | 133. Rolling Mountain | 13,693 | 181. Hayden Peak | 13,561 |
| 86. Mount Spalding | 13,842 | 134. Loveland Mountain | 13,692 | 182. Hagues Peak | 13,560 |
| 87. Hagerman Peak | 13,841 | 135. Wheeler Mountain | 13,690 | 183. Bartlett Mountain | 13,555 |
| 88. Half Peak | 13,841 | 136. Cirque Mountain | 13,686 | 184. Wasatch Mountain | 13,555 |
| 89. Turret Needles | 13,835 | 137. Bald Mountain | 13,684 | 185. Fluted Peak | 13,554 |
| 90. Turret Peak | 13,835 | 138. Mount Oso | 13,684 | 186. McCauley Peak | 13,554 |
| 91. Iowa Peak | 13,831 | 139. White Ridge | 13,684 | 187. Pettingell Peak | 13,553 |
| 92. Jupiter Mountain | 13,830 | 140. Needle Mountains Peak Seven | 13,682 | 188. Tower Mountain | 13,552 |
| 93. Hagged Mountain | 13,824 | 141. Purgatoire Peak | 13,676 | 189. Emma Burr Mountain | 13,544 |
| 94. Mount Silverheels | 13,822 | 142. Mount Tweto | 13,672 | 190. Whitecross Mountain | 13,542 |
| 95. Rio Grande Pyramid | 13,821 | 143. Mount Jackson | 13,670 | 191. Mount Powell | 13,534 |
| 96. Teakettle Mountain | 13,819 | 144. Vestal Peak | 13,664 | 192. Leviathan Peak | 13,528 |
| 97. Dallas Peak | 13,809 | 145. Lookout Peak | 13,661 | 193. Treasure Mountain | 13,528 |
| 98. Niagara Peak | 13,807 | 146. Hamilton Peak | 13,658 | 194. Boulder Mountain | 13,524 |
| 99. Trinity Peaks | 13,805 | 147. Carson Peak | 13,657 | 195. Browns Peak | 13,523 |
| 100. Arrow Peak | 13,803 | 148. Taylor Mountain | 13,657 | 196. Epaulet Mountain | 13,523 |
| 101. Organ Mountain | 13,799 | 149. Coxcomb Peak | 13,656 | 197. Milwaukee Peak | 13,522 |
| 102. Mount Arkansas | 13,795 | 150. Mount Champion | 13,646 | 198. Star Peak | 13,521 |
| 103. Rito Alto Peak | 13,794 | 151. Redcliff | 13,642 | 199. Trinchera Peak | 13,517 |
| 104. Square Top Mountain | 13,794 | 152. Bard Peak | 13,641 | 200. Keefe Peak | 13,516 |
| 105. Animas Mountain | 13,786 | 153. Mount Mamma | 13,634 | 201. Ypsilon Mountain | 13,514 |
| 106. Potosi Peak | 13,786 | 154. Tenmile Range Peak 10 | 13,633 | 202. Mount Marcy | 13,510 |
| 107. Rinker Peak | 13,783 | 155. Mount Silex | 13,628 | 203. Telluride Peak | 13,509 |
| 108. Mosquito Peak | 13,781 | 156. White Dome | 13,627 | 204. Fairchild Mountain | 13,502 |
| 109. Mount Aetna | 13,771 | 157. West Spanish Peak | 13,626 | 205. North Arapaho Peak | 13,502 |
| 110. Ulysses S. Grant Peak | 13,767 | 158. Electric Peak | 13,621 | 206. Pagoda Mountain | 13,497 |
| 111. Bull Hill | 13,761 | 159. The Guardian | 13,617 | 207. Mears Peak | 13,496 |
| 112. Deer Mountain | 13,761 | 160. Father Dyer Peak | 13,615 | 208. Whitehouse Mountain | 13,492 |
| 113. San Miguel Peak | 13,752 | 161. Pico Aislado | 13,611 | 209. Eureka Mountain | 13,489 |
| 114. Storm King Peak | 13,752 | 162. Tijeras Peak | 13,604 | 210. Graystone Peak | 13,489 |
| 115. Mount Sheridan | 13,748 | 163. Gray Wolf Mountain | 13,602 | 211. Cuatro Peak | 13,487 |
| 116. Ptarmigan Peak | 13,739 | 164. Cyclone Mountain | 13,600 | 212. Storm Peak | 13,487 |
| 117. Argentine Peak | 13,738 | 165. Matterhorn Peak | 13,590 | 213. Three Needles | 13,481 |
| 118. Grizzly Peak | 13,738 | 166. Needle Mountains Peak One | 13,589 | 214. Canby Mountain | 13,478 |
| 119. Pilot Knob | 13,738 | 167. Cottonwood Peak | 13,588 | 215. Needle Mountains Peak Three | 13,478 |
| 120. Grizzly Mountain | 13,723 | 168. Mount Emma | 13,581 | 216. Needle Mountains Peak Two | 13,475 |

| Summit | Elevation | Summit | Elevation | Summit | Elevation |
|---|---|---|---|---|---|
| 217. La Junta Peak | 13,472 | 265. Precarious Peak | 13,360 | 313. Pecks Peak | 13,270 |
| 218. Miranda Peak | 13,468 | 266. South Lookout Peak | 13,357 | 314. Antora Peak | 13,266 |
| 219. Mount Ridgeway | 13,468 | 267. Music Mountain | 13,355 | 315. Geneva Peak | 13,266 |
| 220. Treasury Mountain | 13,462 | 268. Hoosier Ridge | 13,352 | 316. Marble Mountain | 13,266 |
| 221. Quail Mountain | 13,461 | 269. Venable Peak | 13,352 | 317. Wildhorse Peak | 13,266 |
| 222. Needle Mountains Peak Eleven | 13,460 | 270. Mount Herard | 13,350 | 318. Knife Point | 13,265 |
| 223. Hanson Peak | 13,454 | 271. Malemute Peak | 13,348 | 319. The Heisspitz | 13,262 |
| 224. Kendall Peak | 13,451 | 272. Peerless Mountain | 13,348 | 320. Middle Peak | 13,261 |
| 225. Horn Peak | 13,450 | 273. Mount White | 13,347 | 321. Darley Mountain | 13,260 |
| 226. Hurricane Peak | 13,447 | 274. Beattie Peak | 13,342 | 322. Whitehead Peak | 13,259 |
| 227. Apache Peak | 13,441 | 275. Brown Mountain | 13,339 | 323. Broken Hill | 13,256 |
| 228. Sleeping Sexton | 13,440 | 276. Kendall Mountain | 13,338 | 324. Fossil Ridge | 13,254 |
| 229. Taylor Peak | 13,435 | 277. Mount Maxwell | 13,335 | 325. Henry Mountain | 13,254 |
| 230. Jenkins Mountain | 13,432 | 278. De Anza Peak | 13,333 | 326. Mount Bancroft | 13,250 |
| 231. Spread Eagle Peak | 13,431 | 279. Twin Peaks | 13,333 | 327. Spring Mountain | 13,244 |
| 232. Gray Needle | 13,430 | 280. Cinnamon Mountain | 13,328 | 328. Landslide Peak | 13,238 |
| 233. Vallecito Mountain | 13,428 | 281. McHenrys Peak | 13,327 | 329. Notch Mountain | 13,237 |
| 234. Grizzly Peak | 13,427 | 282. Storm Peak | 13,326 | 330. Turner Peak | 13,237 |
| 235. Mummy Mountain | 13,425 | 283. West Buffalo Peak | 13,326 | 331. Mount Sniktau | 13,234 |
| 236. Little Giant Peak | 13,416 | 284. Hermit Peak | 13,322 | 332. Belleview Mountain | 13,233 |
| 237. Cleveland Peak | 13,414 | 285. Sunshine Mountain | 13,321 | 333. Hesperus Mountain | 13,232 |
| 238. Needle Mountains Peak Four | 13,410 | 286. Trico Peak | 13,321 | 334. Red Mountain | 13,229 |
| 239. Finnback Knob | 13,409 | 287. Palmyra Peak | 13,319 | 335. Needle Mountains Peak Eight | 13,228 |
| 240. Hilliard Pass | 13,409 | 288. Mount Alice | 13,310 | 336. Mount Audubon | 13,223 |
| 241. Navajo Peak | 13,409 | 289. Aztec Mountain | 13,310 | 337. Macomber Peak | 13,222 |
| 242. Mount Wilcox | 13,408 | 290. Emery Peak | 13,310 | 338. Eagle Peak | 13,221 |
| 243. Mariquita Peak | 13,405 | 291. Echo Mountain | 13,309 | 339. Jones Mountain | 13,221 |
| 244. Needle Mountains Peak Nine | 13,402 | 292. Waverly Mountain | 13,309 | 340. Greenhalgh Mountain | 13,220 |
| 245. Mount Rhoda | 13,402 | 293. Mount Warren | 13,307 | 341. Engineer Mountain | 13,218 |
| 246. Baldy Chato | 13,401 | 294. Geissler Mountain | 13,301 | 342. Irving Peak | 13,218 |
| 247. South Arapaho Peak | 13,397 | 295. Summit Peak | 13,300 | 343. Thirsty Peak | 13,217 |
| 248. Bent Peak | 13,393 | 296. James Peak | 13,294 | 344. Red Peak | 13,215 |
| 249. Parry Peak | 13,391 | 297. Electric Peak | 13,292 | 345. Fairview Peak | 13,214 |
| 250. Rogers Peak | 13,391 | 298. Sheep Mountain | 13,292 | 346. Campbell Peak | 13,213 |
| 251. Mount Owen | 13,387 | 299. Dolores Peak | 13,290 | 347. Homestake Peak | 13,209 |
| 252. Chicago Peak | 13,385 | 300. Needle Mountains Peak Sixteen | 13,290 | 348. Powell Peak | 13,208 |
| 253. Baldy Cinco | 13,383 | 301. Bonita Peak | 13,286 | 349. Teocalli Mountain | 13,208 |
| 254. Lakes Peak | 13,382 | 302. Needle Mountains Peak Five | 13,283 | 350. Ellingwood Ridge | 13,206 |
| 255. De Anza Peak | 13,380 | 303. Truro Peak | 13,282 | 351. Hayden Mountain | 13,206 |
| 256. Italian Mountain | 13,378 | 304. Grizzly Peak | 13,281 | 352. Jacque Peak | 13,205 |
| 257. Monumental Peak | 13,375 | 305. Mount Lady Washington | 13,281 | 353. Mount Nebo | 13,205 |
| 258. Dome Mountain | 13,370 | 306. Galena Mountain | 13,278 | 354. Bennett Peak | 13,203 |
| 259. Mount Guyot | 13,370 | 307. Comanche Peak | 13,277 | 355. Tuttle Mountain | 13,203 |
| 260. Sultan Mountain | 13,368 | 308. Ruby Mountain | 13,277 | 356. Lenawee Mountain | 13,201 |
| 261. Gold Dust Peak | 13,365 | 309. Kiowa Peak | 13,276 | 357. Hagar Mountain | 13,195 |
| 262. Engelmann Peak | 13,362 | 310. Mendoza Peak | 13,275 | 358. Tenmile Range Peak 9 | 13,195 |
| 263. Pearl Mountain | 13,362 | 311. Seigal Mountain | 13,274 | 359. London Mountain | 13,194 |
| 264. Iron Nipple | 13,360 | 312. Whitney Peak | 13,271 | 360. Mount Moss | 13,192 |

**Appendix C • 500 Highest Named Summits in Colorado**

| Summit | Elevation | Summit | Elevation | Summit | Elevation |
| --- | --- | --- | --- | --- | --- |
| 361. Red Peak | 13,189 | 409. Eagles Nest | 13,091 | 457. West Sheridan | 12,962 |
| 362. Sheep Mountain | 13,188 | 410. Paiute Peak | 13,088 | 458. Purple Mountain | 12,958 |
| 363. King Solomon Mountain | 13,185 | 411. Virginia Peak | 13,088 | 459. Ouray Peak | 12,957 |
| 364. Mount Valois | 13,185 | 412. Emerson Mountain | 13,085 | 460. Clark Peak | 12,951 |
| 365. Beaubien Peak | 13,184 | 413. Keller Mountain | 13,085 | 461. Desolation Peaks | 12,949 |
| 366. Rowe Mountain | 13,184 | 414. Boreas Mountain | 13,082 | 462. East Ball Mountain | 12,947 |
| 367. Bullion Mountain | 13,182 | 415. Whale Peak | 13,078 | 463. Fools Peak | 12,947 |
| 368. Collier Mountain | 13,180 | 416. Snowdon Peak | 13,077 | 464. Vasquez Peak | 12,947 |
| 369. Santa Fe Peak | 13,180 | 417. Winfield Peak | 13,077 | 465. Calico Mountain | 12,944 |
| 370. Copeland Mountain | 13,176 | 418. Florida Mountain | 13,076 | 466. Pawnee Peak | 12,943 |
| 371. Conejos Peak | 13,172 | 419. North Twilight Peak | 13,075 | 467. Star Mountain | 12,941 |
| 372. Sheep Mountain | 13,168 | 420. Mount Garfield | 13,074 | 468. Mount Richthofen | 12,940 |
| 373. Amherst Mountain | 13,165 | 421. Blackwall Mountain | 13,073 | 469. Woods Mountain | 12,940 |
| 374. Mount Helen | 13,164 | 422. Sheep Mountain | 13,070 | 470. Clover Mountain | 12,935 |
| 375. Kelso Mountain | 13,164 | 423. Mount Chiquita | 13,069 | 471. Little Bartlett Mountain | 12,935 |
| 376. Twilight Peak | 13,158 | 424. Hunts Peak | 13,067 | 472. Crystal Peak | 12,933 |
| 377. Baldy Mountain | 13,155 | 425. Centennial Park | 13,062 | 473. Tenmile Peak | 12,933 |
| 378. Taylor Peak | 13,153 | 426. Middle Mountain | 13,060 | 474. Yellow Mountain | 12,933 |
| 379. Arikaree Peak | 13,150 | 427. Mount Owen | 13,058 | 475. Dolly Varden Mountain | 12,932 |
| 380. Montezuma Peak | 13,150 | 428. Van Wirt Mountain | 13,056 | 476. Sunshine Mountain | 12,930 |
| 381. Point Pun | 13,150 | 429. Houghton Mountain | 13,052 | 477. Eureka Mountain | 12,929 |
| 382. Babcock Peak | 13,149 | 430. Lambertson Peak | 13,051 | 478. Mount Julian | 12,928 |
| 383. South River Peak | 13,149 | 431. Green Mountain | 13,049 | 479. Stones Peak | 12,922 |
| 384. Grand Turk | 13,148 | 432. West Dyer Mountain | 13,047 | 480. Round Mountain | 12,912 |
| 385. Precipice Peak | 13,144 | 433. West Needle Mountain | 13,045 | 481. Cross Mountain | 12,911 |
| 386. Little Horn Peak | 13,143 | 434. Eagle Peak | 13,043 | 482. Larson Peak | 12,908 |
| 387. Willoughby Mountain | 13,142 | 435. Wolcott Mountain | 13,041 | 483. Simpson Mountain | 12,904 |
| 388. Robeson Peak | 13,140 | 436. Gladstone Ridge | 13,038 | 484. Ganley Mountain | 12,902 |
| 389. Pomeroy Mountain | 13,139 | 437. United States Mountain | 13,036 | 485. Galena Mountain | 12,893 |
| 390. Savage Peak | 13,139 | 438. West Elk Peak | 13,035 | 486. Ute Ridge | 12,893 |
| 391. Ogalalla Peak | 13,138 | 439. Organ Mountain | 13,022 | 487. South Peak | 12,892 |
| 392. Hunchback Mountain | 131,36 | 440. Chief Mountain | 13,014 | 488. Decatur Mountain | 12,890 |
| 393. Francisco Peak | 13,135 | 441. Hope Mountain | 13,012 | 489. Red Mountain No 3 | 12,890 |
| 394. Sullivan Mountain | 13,134 | 442. Pennsylvania Mountain | 13,006 | 490. Breckinridge Peak | 12,889 |
| 395. Mount Flora | 13,132 | 443. Ruffner Mountain | 13,003 | 491. Revenue Mountain | 12,889 |
| 396. Mount Eva | 13,130 | 444. Overlook Point | 12,998 | 492. Witter Peak | 12,884 |
| 397. Lomo Liso Mountain | 13,128 | 445. Greenback Mountain | 12,997 | 493. Mount George | 12,876 |
| 398. Mount Kennedy | 13,125 | 446. Bear Mountain | 12,987 | 494. Len Shoemaker Ridge | 12,875 |
| 399. Fitzpatrick Peak | 13,124 | 447. Hayden Peak | 12,987 | 495. Mount Logan | 12,871 |
| 400. Spiller Peak | 13,123 | 448. Tenmile Range Peak 8 | 12,987 | 496. Buckeye Peak | 12,867 |
| 401. Peters Peak | 13,122 | 449. Vulcan Mountain | 12,987 | 497. State Line Peak | 12,867 |
| 402. Mount Kreutzer | 13,120 | 450. Square Top Mountain | 12,985 | 498. Long Trek Mountain | 12,866 |
| 403. Isolation Peak | 13,118 | 451. Middle Mountain | 12,984 | 499. Tenmile Range Peak 4 | 12,866 |
| 404. McClellan Mountain | 13,117 | 452. Little Baldy Mountain | 12,982 | 500. Mount Niehardt | 12,863 |
| 405. Lizard Head | 13,113 | 453. Mount Toll | 12,979 | | |
| 406. Thunder Mountain | 13,108 | 454. Red Mountain | 12,974 | | |
| 407. Bushnell Peak | 13,105 | 455. Engineer Mountain | 12,968 | | |
| 408. Middle Mountain | 13,100 | 456. Shoshoni Peak | 12,967 | | |

# *Appendix D*

## Safe Mountain Travel

This appendix offers a few cautions to aid you in safe mountain travel. You also will find an introduction to exploring the mountains by back road and by foot, one of the most enjoyable ways. Many other good books can be found in Colorado bookstores to assist in planning your adventures.

### Mountain Weather

The old saying that "if you don't like the weather, just wait five minutes and it will change" is particularly true in Colorado. The weather is very unpredictable especially in the high mountains. It can snow in the mountains any month of the year. Thunderstorms move in quickly, especially on summer afternoons. Lightning can be very hazardous, so keep an eye out for fast-moving storms. Get off ridges or peaks and avoid tall or lone objects. Mountains and ridges may obstruct your view of quickly approaching storms.

### Altitude Sickness

This may occur at levels above 8,000 feet (2,400 m) for people who are not acclimatized to the higher altitudes. Symptoms include headache, nausea, dizziness, or shortness of breath. If symptoms occur, drink additional liquids, move slowly, use aspirin, and breathe deeply. If symptoms persist, descend to a lower altitude as soon as you can.

It can take several days to adjust to higher altitudes, but you can reduce the chance of altitude sickness by limiting strenuous activity, drinking plenty of fluids, and eating lightly. Avoid cigarettes and alcohol, which can intensify the effects of altitude sickness. If you have a heart or lung condition, high altitudes may affect you more.

# General Safety Tips

**Giardiasis** – This is an intestinal disorder caused by parasites in the water. No water should be consumed from Colorado streams except at designated areas. If untreated water must be consumed, it should be boiled or filtered before use.

**Animals** – Some of the animals found in Colorado mountains include black bear, elk, moose, mountain lion, snowshoe hare, beaver, pika, marmot, and ptarmigan. Please use caution if you encounter animals. Some may attack humans if they feel threatened. Do not feed birds or animals. Some of them can be quite friendly, and they may even beg for food. Feeding them only encourages dependence on humans and disturbs the natural ecosystems.

**Climbing** – Climbing is a technical sport that requires extensive training. Do not attempt to climb unless you have the required skill and equipment. Special permits may be required in some areas of the state.

**Clothing** – Even in the middle of summer, when it's warm and balmy down on the plains, the temperatures and winds in the mountains can be freezing. You should always carry extra clothing.

# Driving Tips

While driving steep mountain roads, keep your air conditioner turned off, it can strain your car's cooling system. When descending steep mountain grades, don't ride the brake pedal—this can lead to overheating and possible brake failure. Even with an automatic transmission, use a lower gear to help reduce your speed. The following emergency equipment should be carried in the vehicle:

| | |
|---|---|
| shovel | sand or cat litter (for traction) |
| candles and matches | extra food |
| extra clothing | blankets or sleeping bag |

# Essential Equipment for Hikers

When venturing into the mountains on foot, it is extremely important to be prepared for unforeseen circumstances and emergencies. It doesn't matter if you're going on an afternoon walk in the woods or a multi-day backpack—always carry this essential equipment for safe backcountry travel:

| | |
|---|---|
| flashlight | (with spare batteries and bulb) |
| matches | (in a waterproof container along with fire starter) |
| extra clothing | (including space blanket & large plastic garbage bags for emergency shelter) |

map
compass
extra food
knife
first-aid kit containing:

| | | |
|---|---|---|
| sewing needle | aspirin | anti-bacterial ointment |
| antiseptic swabs | butterfly bandages | adhesive tape |
| Band-Aids | gauze pads | triangular bandages |
| moleskin | roll of 3 inch gauze | first-aid instructions |

# Optional Equipment

Other equipment you may wish to take:

| | | |
|---|---|---|
| pack/hip pouch | camera/film | binoculars |
| field guides | trail books | sunglasses |
| candle | safety pins | wire for repairs |
| signal mirror | fire starter | aluminum foil |
| water tablets | space blanket | flares |
| tape | suntan lotion | lip protection |
| insect repellent | toilet paper | nylon cord/rope |
| notebook/pencils | watch | towel |
| water filter | repair kit(s) | rain gear |
| personal-hygiene articles | | |

# Glossary

**alpine ecosystem**
The life zone of plants and animals living above treeline. In Colorado, this starts above approximately 11,500 feet (3,500 meters).

**bedrock**
Unweathered rock beneath the surface soil.

**bedding plane**
A layer of bedrock beneath the surface soil.

**cirque**
A bowl-shaped depression high on a mountain, carved by glacial action.

**couloir**
A steep mountain gully.

**Continental Divide**
The dividing line running north and south along the continent, from which water will run either west to the Pacific Ocean or east to the Atlantic Ocean.

**gneiss**
A banded metamorphic rock with layers of minerals.

**hogback**
A geological feature formed when the caprock tilts at a steep angle to the underlying bedrock.

**igneous rock**
Rock that is produced under intense heat. One of the three basic types of rocks.

**lateral moraine**
A ridge of earth and rocks deposited to the side of a glacier.

**massif** A French word for "massive" which describes a cluster of mountains that rise above the surrounding low-lying ground.

**metamorphic rock**
Rock that has undergone structural change. One of the three basic types of rocks.

**montane ecosystem**
The life zone of plants and animals residing at 6,000 to 9,000 feet (1,800 to 2,750 meters).

**moraine**
A ridge or mound of dirt, rocks, and gravel deposited by a glacier.

**orogeny**
The collision of continental plates in the earth's crust which builds mountains.

**pass**
A low point connecting two or more parts of a mountain range.

**permafrost**
Permanently frozen subsoil.

**ridge**
A narrow, elongated crest that is part of a mountain or hill.

**saddle**
A ridge that forms a low point connecting two summits.

**schist**
Metamorphic rock with a crystalline structure composed of layers of minerals that are easily split.

**sedimentary rock** Sediment deposited in layers that become compressed and transformed into rock. One of the three basic types of rock.

**subalpine ecosystem**
The life zone of plants and animals residing at 9,000 to 11,500 feet (2,750 to 3,500 meters).

**treeline**
The elevation (about 11,500 feet, or 3,500 meters, in Colorado), above which no trees will grow.

**tundra**
An ecosystem of plants residing above treeline in the mountains or the arctic regions of the world.

# *Bibliography*

Arps, Louisa Ward, ed. 1962. *Front range panorama.*
 [Denver]: Colorado Mountain Club.

Arps, Louisa Ward, and Elinor E. Kingery. 1966. *High country names.*
 Denver: Colorado Mountain Club.

Arps, Louisa Ward, and Elinor E. Kingery. 1972. *High country names.* Rev. ed.
 Estes Park, Colo.: Rocky Mountain Nature Association.

Banks, Jim. 1964. Outdoors at the Air Force academy. *Trail and Timberline* 548
(August): 127-130.

Bartlett, Richard A. 1962. *Great surveys of the American west.*
Norman, Okla.: University of Oklahoma Press.

Borneman, Walter R. 1984. *Colorado's other mountains: A climbing guide to selected
peaks under 14,000 feet.* N.p.: Cordillera Press.

Borneman, Walter R., and Lyndon Lampert. 1978. *A climbing guide to Colorado's
fourteeners.* 2d ed. Boulder: Pruett Publishing.

Bright, William. 1993. *Colorado place name*s. Boulder: Johnson Books.

Caughey, Bruce, and Dean Winstanley. 1991. *The Colorado guide.* Rev. ed.
Golden Colo.: Fulcrum Publishing.

Chronic, Halka. 1980. *Roadside geology of Colorado.*
Missoula, Mont.: Mountain Press Publishing.

(Colorado Mountain Club, Pikes Peak Group). 1933. *Trail and Timberline* 179
(Sepember): 130.

Colorado Writers Project. [1941] 1943. *Colorado: a guide to the highest state.*
New York: Hastings House.

Cummings, Lewis A. ed. 1947. *History of the Spanish Peaks Ranger District*
Reprint, N. p.

Eichler, Geo R. 1977. *Colorado place names.* Boulder: Johnson Publishing.

Edrinn, Roger. 1991 *Colorado fourteeners: grand slam.*
Fort Collins, Colo.: Above the Timber.

Foster, Mike. 1988. Modesty, thy name is Parry. *Trail and Timberline* 830
(July/August): unk.

Green, Stewart M. 1994. *Colorado scenic drives.* Helena Mont.: Falcon Press.

Hagen, Mary, ed. 1984. *Larimer County Place Names.*
Fort Collins Colo.: Old Army Press.

Hart, John L. J. [1931]. *Fourteen thousand feet: A history of the naming and early
ascents of the high Colorado peaks.* Reprint 1972. [Denver]: Colorado Mountain Club.

Hodge, Frederick Webb. 1969. *Handbook of American Indians north of Mexico.*
Reprint. New York: Greenwood Press Publishing.

Huerfano butte: a historic site. 1952. *Trail and Timberline* 248 (August): 107-108.

Jacobs, Randy, ed. 1992. *Guide to the Colorado mountains*. 9th ed. Denver: Colorado Mountain Club.

Koch, Don. 1987. *The Colorado pass book*. 2d ed. Boulder: Pruett Publishing.

Kramarsic, Joe. 1988. Fishers peak: Raton pass landmark. *Trail and Timberline* 826 (March): 68-69.

Lecompte, Janet. 1978. *Pueblo, Hardscrabble, Greenhorn, The upper Arkansas, 1832-1856*. Norman Okla: University of Oklahoma Press.

Malocsay, Zoltan. 1983. *Hikers guide: Pikes Peak and South Park region*. Colorado Springs: Century One Press.

Matthews, Ruth Eselle. 1940. *A study of Colorado place names*. Thesis: Stanford University.

Mayhew, Susan and Anne Penny. 1992. *The concise Oxford dictionary of geography*. Oxford, N.Y.: Oxford University Press.

Mctighe, James. 1984. *Roadside history of Colorado*. Boulder: Johnson Books.

Ormes, Robert M. [unk]. Nomenclature file. Colorado Mountain Club.

Ormes, Robert M. 1967. *Colorado skylines. Vol. I, Front Range from the east*. [Colorado Springs]: Unk.

Ormes, Robert M. 1969. *Colorado skylines. Vol. II, the parks*. [Colorado Springs]: Unk.

Ormes, Robert M. 1971. *Colorado skylines. Vol. III, Colorado River basin*. [Colorado Springs]: Unk.

Ormes, Robert M. 1974. *Colorado skylines. Vol. IV, southern section*. [Colorado Springs]: Unk.

Osterwald, Doris B. 1989. *Rocky mountain splendor*. Lakewood Colo.: Western Guideways.

Pearl, Richard M. 1972. *Colorado gem trails and mineral guide*. Rev. 3rd. ed. unk.: Swallow Press/Ohio University.

Pearl, Richard M. 1975. *Landforms of Colorado*. Colorado Springs: Earth Science Publishing.

Pekinik, George. 1992. *The Cheyenne cañon and Broadmoor guidebook and almanac*. Colorado Springs: Hoopoe Publications.

Rennicke, Jeff. 1986. *Colorado Mountain Ranges*. Helena, Mont.: Falcon Press.

Rogers, James Grafton. [unk]. Colorado geographic place names. Denver: Colorado Historical Society. Microfilms.

Skiff, Carl, ed. 1977. *Colorado's highest*. Silverton, Colo.: Sundance Publications.

Smith, Phyllis. 1993. *Weather pioneers: the Signal Corps station at Pikes Peak*. Athens, Ohio: Ohio University Press.

Sporleder, Louis B. 1960. *The romance of the Spanish Peaks*. [Pueblo, Colo.]: O'Brien Printing and Stationery.

Tatum, R. M. 1946. *Geology of the Trinidad region*. Southwestern Lore (December).

Taylor, Morris F. 1959. *A sketch of early days on the Purgatory*. Trinidad, Colo.: Risley Printing.

Taylor, Morris F. 1966. *Trinidad, Colorado territory*. Pueblo, Colo.: O'Brien Printing and Stationery.

Taylor, Ralph C. 1963. *Colorado south of the border*. Denver: Sage Books.

Thessen, Michael. 1991. *Trail guide: Sangre de Cristo mountains*. Pueblo, Colo.: Wild Images.

Thomas, Chauncey. 1925. Mountains tales. *Outdoor Life* (October): 278

U.S. Geological Survey National Mapping Division. 1994. *Geographic names information system: digital gazetteer*. N.p.: U.S. Department of the Interior.

U.S. Geological Survey. 1980. 1:500,000 Colorado topographic map. Rev.

U.S. Geological Survey. [various]. 1:250,000 Colorado topographic map series. Rev.

U.S. Geological Survey. [various]. 1:100,000 Colorado topographic map series. Rev.

U.S. Geological Survey. [various]. 1:50,000 Colorado topographic map series. Rev.

Walther, Lou. 1983. *Golden Trails*. Boulder: Johnson Publishing Co.

Young, Caroline. 1952. Huerfano butte monument. *Trail and Timberline*. 402 (June): 97.

# Index

# About the Author

Joe Milligan is a writer, outdoor photographer, and avid Colorado mountaineer. Joe has been very active in the Colorado Mountain Club, serving several years on the board of directors. He also has served as the Colorado Mountain Club's Pikes Peak Group chairman and conservation chairman. He is a member of the International Association of Panoramic Photographers and the Colorado Historical Society. *PeakFinders Roadside Guide to the Colorado Mountains: Interstate 25 Skylines* is his first book. Joe is currently working on the five or six other volumes in the *Roadside Guide to the Colorado Mountains* series. Look for them soon in your favorite book store.

Joe lives in Colorado Springs with his wife, Marcy, their four children, and three cats. When he isn't at his computer writing about the Colorado mountains, Joe is out exploring, photographing, and just plain enjoying them.

GUIDE
BOOKS

*Peak* Finders™

# Look for the upcoming
## *Roadside Guide to the Colorado Mountains:*
## *Interstate 70*

### PeakFinders™ Roadside Guide to the Colorado Mountains: Interstate 70

- Complete coverage of Colorado Interstate 70 from the Utah-Colorado border to the Great Plains east of Denver.
- Complete coverage of the ski resorts located along I-70.

### Other Guidebooks Coming in 1997:

- PeakFinders™ Roadside Guide to the Colorado Mountains: Highway 550
- PeakFinders™ Roadside Guide to the Colorado Mountains: Highway 285
- PeakFinders™ Roadside Guide to the Colorado Mountains: Highway 50
- PeakFinders™ Roadside Guide to the Colorado Mountains: Highway 40
- PeakFinders™ Roadside Guide to the Colorado Mountains: Highway 160

See your local bookseller or contact:

Westcliffe Publishers, Inc. • 2650 South Zuni Street • Englewood, Colorado 80110 • (303) 935-0900